AA ★★   RAC ★★

Glenspean Lodge Hotel, Roy Bridge
INVERNESS-SHIRE
Telephone SPEAN BRIDGE 224

The hotel stands in its own grounds 2 miles east of Roy Bridge on the A84 overlooking Monessie Gorge. The hotel is warm and tastefully decorated with an excellent cuisine. Shooting and fishing are available by arrangement and there are unrivalled opportunities in the neighbourhood for hill walking and rock climbing. There are laundry and good drying facilities available to guests.

Resident Proprietors: Mr & Mrs NEAL MACPHERSON SMITH

Photo: *Hamish M. Brown*

Skye, The Old Man of Storr and Satellites

THE SCOTTISH

MOUNTAINEERING

CLUB JOURNAL

| VOL. XXXI | 1978 | No. 169 |

THE SCOTTISH HAUTE ROUTE

By David Grieve

CONCEPTION.

THE GROWTH of interest in ski mountaineering as a sport has led to the establishment in several different countries of high level ski routes, e.g. the Classic Haute Route from Chamonix to Zermatt, a Norwegian Haute Route, even a Moroccan Haute Route. The intention of this article is to establish a Scottish Haute Route and to describe what is believed to be its first successful completion.

Previously various attempts to traverse the Highlands on ski have been made but all seem to have been frustrated by bad weather or other factors. One notable effort backed by the B.B.C. is said to have foundered in the fleshpots of the Coylum Bridge Hotel!

In general terms any true Haute Route requires to follow an E–W line including Nevis in the West and the high Grampians in the East. West of Drumochter the mountain spine is interrupted by Lochs Treig and Ericht and unless one has a boat laid on these obstacles force detours from the direct line.

East of Drumochter, in the vicinity of Gaick the Grampians divide into two lobes on either side of the Geldie and Dee valleys. The southern lobe extends along the broad ridge including An Sgarsoch, Beinn Iutharn Mhór, Glas Maol, Lochnagar and Mount Keen while the northern encompasses the Cairngorms proper. Either provides a satisfactory high level route but our own choice was with the northern lobe because it took in the Cairngorms, thus not only providing a more challenging route in the technical sense but also incorporating the two highest mountain ranges in Scotland and truly deserving the title of the Scottish Haute Route.

The precise staging and detail selection of the route is open to a good deal of variation and no doubt weather conditions and the energies of different parties would produce differing bags of peaks traversed en route. One factor which dominates however, is the distribution of mountain bothies and the need to base one's plans on

their availability.   Much of the Scottish character of the whole
venture arises from the use of these splendid shelters and we often
found ourselves giving a vote of thanks to the Mountain Bothies
Association for their efforts in this direction.

Other considerations required, were a line which was as straight
and uncontrived as possible, no break in continuity of the route or
reliance on mechanical transport, suitable provision for modification
or escape if conditions warranted and finally a route which could be
completed within the span of a week's holiday, with luck and
perseverance.

Our Scottish Haute Route starts in Deeside at Crathie and follows
a virtually straight line across the Highlands for one hundred miles
(163 km.) to finish at Fort William. It may be done equally well in
the opposite direction.

In more detail, there are six more or less equal stages as follows:—

Approach: Crathie to Corndavon Lodge (9 km., 2 km. of which by
car if the road is open).

Stage I: Corndavon Lodge – Ben Avon, Beinn a Bhuird – Hutchison
Hut in Choire Etchachan (24 km.).

Stage II: Hutchison Hut – Ben Macdui, Lairig Ghru, Cairn Toul,
Moine Mór – Ruigh-aiteachan Bothy in Glen Feshie (25 km.).

Stage III: Ruigh-aiteachan – Carn Dearg Mór, Tromie Dam, Carn
na Caim – Dalwhinnie (29 km.).

Stage IV: Dalwhinnie – The Fara, Culra Lodge, Ben Alder – Ben
Alder Cottage (26 km.).

Stage V: Ben Alder Cottage – Sgòr Gaibhre, Corrour Lodge, Beinn na
Lap – Staoineag Bothy (26 km.).

Stage VI: Staoineag Bothy – (Sgùrr Choinnich Mór) Aonach Beag,
Carn Mór Dearg, Ben Nevis – Fort William (24 km.).

This was our conception of the Haute Route.   In fact, bad
weather led to it being done in seven stages instead of six, as will be
described.

OBSERVATIONS AND EQUIPMENT.

The following comments may be helpful to others who wish to do
the Route.

Ideally there should be complete *snow cover* from coast to coast.
In practice this happens rarely and one should be prepared to carry
skis across low ground connecting the main sections.

The decision to travel *eastward or westward* can only be made in
the light of weather patterns or predictions. Expected wind direction
is a major factor but there is much to be said for a fine weather start
from Nevis where ski-ing in bad visibility may be difficult and even
dangerous.

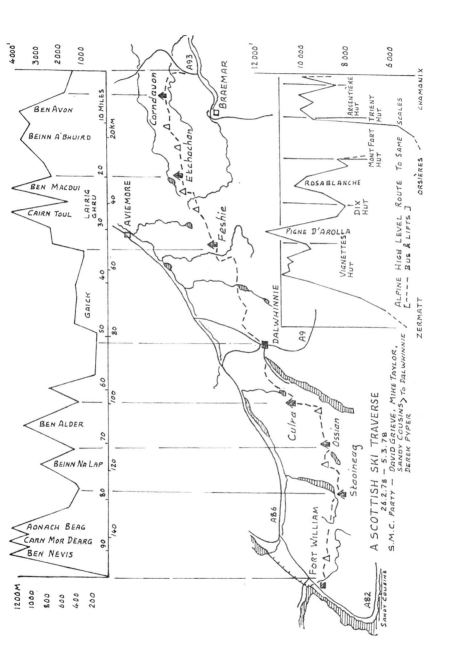

A SCOTTISH SKI TRAVERSE
26.2.78 – 5.3.78
S.M.C. PARTY — DAVID GRIEVE, MIKE TAYLOR,
SANDY COUSINS> TO DALWHINNIE
DEREK PYPER

Emergencies—Parties should be ready to bivouac if need be and able to provide adequate repairs to ski equipment and first aid for such accidents as a broken leg. The route takes one out of touch with civilisation for up to three days at a time so rapid rescue cannot be expected. In fact firm arrangements may have to be made to avoid alarms being raised and premature rescue being enforced.

Wet Weather probably poses as great a hazard as blizzard conditions so adequate protective clothing is needed. One of our group had a suit of the new Goretex clothing and was able to stay pretty well dry throughout.

Navigation, etc.—White-out conditions were encountered several times and demanded great care. It is even easier to go over a cornice on ski than on foot. We used a Thommen altimeter and found it a valuable aid.

Weight—The need to carry axe, crampons and a lightweight rope (we used 100 ft. of 6 mm.) and to be self sufficient in bothies (food, cooking equipment, sleeping bags and spare clothes) made weight a major consideration. We were unable to get below 30 lbs. (14 Kg.) although we planted several food caches to provide culinary luxury and lighten our packs. A good modern pack frame rucksack sits better when ski-ing downhill, sweats less under the back and has a useful selection of pockets—an improvement over the traditional Joe Brown type sack. Worthwhile extras we carried were a tiny radio for weather forecasts and a 4 oz. handsaw for cutting up firewood.

Ski Equipment—Langlauf skis are excellent for fast cross-country work in good snow conditions but we considered them unsuitable for several sections of our Haute Route where pleasurable ski-ing would only be possible with downhill gear. Heavy packs further reduce the advantages of Langlauf skis. We recommend 'Compact' skis which have the great advantage of being shorter and more easily carried on a rucksack, preferably specialist off piste models such as the Rossignol 'Choucas.'

Bindings such as the Vinersa which give an option of complete heel lift are a substantial improvement on those with a more limited uplift like the Marker. This is especially the case on the flat or gently sloping terrain so typically encountered in Scottish ski mountaineering. Skins which stick on are much better than those with straps, in terms of weight, efficiency in use and speed of handling.

Harcheisen (ski crampons) were a decided asset on steep or icy slopes. Boots should not only give good ski-ing control but also accept crampons and be suitable for walking.

EXECUTION.

The idea of attempting the Scottish Haute Route was discussed at the S.M.C. Dinner in December, 1977. During January, arrangements were finalised and late February was chosen as the most suitable time. This proved an unfortunate choice because the first half of February produced a nearly ideal combination of heavy snowfall followed by fine weather. On Sunday, 26th February, four days after the thaw set in, the party assembled at Dalwhinnie. Sandy Cousins and I drove down from Aviemore and Mike Taylor and Derek Pyper arrived from Braemar via Kirkmichael. The weather was discouraging to say the least, with thick mist and penetrating drizzle. At one o'clock, the weather report predicted brighter weather in the East and so it was decided to do the trip from East to West. Mike Taylor's Saab was left in Dalwhinnie with spare gear and food in it. The other car was loaded up and driven to Deeside over the Devil's Elbow. Deep snow still blocked the Gairnshiel road just above Crathie, so this was the enforced departure point. After final packing and distribution of communal gear, the car was driven back to Aberdeen by the support party in the person of Madeleine Grieve.

The expedition then set out on ski, through the mist to Corndavon Lodge, arriving there shortly after dark. Although the Lodge is largely in ruins, there remain a stable and bothy in excellent condition. Abundant firewood was to hand and a fine steak supper was shortly washed down by a bottle of claret, in front of a roaring fire. Everyone rated this a suitably auspicious start and Corndavon a five-star bothy.

DAY ONE.

Overnight, clearing skies led to a hard frost. When we set off at 7.30 the following morning, the weather was perfect, the snow was crunchy and Glen Gairn was looking absolutely great. Progress up the long shoulder of Ben Avon was slow and laborious due to unaccustomed heavy packs. Once on the plateau progress was easier. The weird summit tors were encrusted with snow and the plateau surface contorted with sastrugi. Descending to the Sneck on excellent snow we had fine views of the Garbh Choire and Mitre Ridge. Windswept slopes above the Col forced a short ski carry and in deteriorating weather, Cnap a Chléirich was skirted on the North side. Map and compass had to be used to locate the North top of Beinn a Bhuird in a surprisingly sudden and complete whiteout. The descent from the summit to the Yellow Moss is three kilometres in length and in clearing mist we had full advantage of this fine run. A motion to climb Beinn a Chaorainn was not seconded and so we crossed the Yellow Moss in a westerly direction before dropping steeply down to the Lairig an Laoigh. From this point a long descending traverse below the cliffs of Beinn Mheadhoin, crossing massive avalanche debris, led without further effort to the Hutchison Memorial Hut in Choire Etchachan. (Ten hours from Corndavon Lodge).

A food bag buried earlier in the season was retrieved slightly the worse for wear. Suffice to say that of Scotland's traditional products, whisky keeps better underground than oatcakes! The Hutchison Hut is a very bare bothy and was by far the least comfortable of all the overnight stops on the trip.

DAY TWO.

The next day dawned cold and cheerless and the cliffs of the corrie were veiled in thick mist. We set out at seven o'clock in a persistent drizzle which turned to snow about the level of Loch Etchachan. There was little wind and zero visibility. All our navigational skills were eventually required to locate the summit of Ben Macdhui. In this respect, mention must be made of the value of the Thommen altimeter. On this occasion and subsequently it allowed pinpoint accuracy in route finding under the most adverse conditions. From the summit the Tailors' Burn was located and descended in thick mist down to the 800 metre level. This was bad luck, because the snow was superb for ski-ing and the poor visibility prevented full enjoyment of what must be one of the finest ski descents in Scotland. The snow was continuous to the floor of the Lairig where we lunched, four hours after leaving the hut. After crossing the Dee on a substantial snow bridge, a long diagonal ascent led through the mist to the lip of the Soldiers' Coire. From this point, a series of steep zig-zags took us to the foot of the South East Summit ridge of Cairn Toul. This was ascended on foot, giving an exhilarating and interesting ridge climb. There was perfect snow again for the run off Cairn Toul and this time the weather cleared in time to enjoy it. Direct vision simplified the descent to Loch nan Cnapan and the crossing of the Moine Mhór where the deep trough of Glen Einich and the huge buttressed face of the Sgòran Dubhs opened before us. It was a long slog round the head of Coire Garbhlach and a relief to reach the head of the Allt Coire Chaoil. This was well filled with snow and gave a good run to well below the tree line as darkness was falling. A rather weary party made its way by torchlight through the Feshie forest to Ruigh-aiteachan Bothy. (12½ hours from the Etchachan Hut). This was another first class bothy and before long a roaring fire with food and other refreshments from the second food cache restored us all to high spirits.

DAY THREE.

The section from Glen Feshie to Dalwhinnie had been regarded as a fairly easy day on lower ground. Low cloud and rain at 8 a.m. led to the traverse of Carn Dearg Mór being abandoned. Instead the day started with a short walk carrying skis through the woods of Glen Feshie. Then the route followed an interesting glen past Lochan an t'Sluie to the water shed. From here we contoured round the south side of the Tromie basin, keeping above the snow line, to reach the

Tromie Dam below Lochan an t'Seilich. Unfortunately as the day progressed, the weather deteriorated steadily. By lunchtime an easterly gale was blowing great sheets of sleety rain across the mountain sides. It was clearly impractical to traverse either Carn na Caim or Meall Chuaich and so an escape route was selected through the pass between them. A snow-filled Land Rover track down the Allt Coire Chuaich gave an excellent ski descent almost to Loch Cuaich. The final eight kilometre walk alongside the Aqueduct to Dalwhinnie was an unpleasant experience. The weight of skis on rucksacks was greatly exaggerated by the gale force wind while the rain continued unremittingly. Darkness fell as the lights of Dalwhinnie appeared in the distance and the final stretch was again by torchlight. (11 hours from Glen Feshie).

The conditions experienced on this section were arguably the most dangerous we encountered. The chilling effect of gale and rain must not be underestimated. Once wet, stops to rest and eat became inadequate because of the rapid chilling. The tendency to press on quickly in order to keep warm increased fatigue and exhaustion/exposure was perhaps already taking effect.

The transport café at Dalwhinnie can be given an unreserved recommendation—it is clean, warm, comfortable and cheap and gave us the chance to get all our clothes dried.

DAY FOUR.

There was no change in the weather the following day and no one was keen to set off for Ben Alder. Thus the programme fell one day behind. This created problems for Derek and Sandy who were obliged to start work on the Monday. Reluctantly it was decided to split the party and Derek and Sandy obligingly offered to drive the Saab over to Fort William. After a large transport café lunch Mike and I left at 2 p.m. bound for Culra Lodge. The gale was moderating somewhat and the rain becoming intermittent. A short climb above Loch Ericht led into a snow filled gully taking us into the upper corrie and finally on to the ridge of The Fara. This was a quite delightful ridge, with good snow cover and impressive views into steep corries, with Loch Ericht and Ben Alder Lodge far below. After Meall Cruaidh a good run down stopped just short of the tin garage at Pattack. With firewood from the forest, the sacks were heavy for the last few kilometres' walk across to Culra Lodge, reached shortly after dark. It was well worthwhile however, to have a cheerful fire and dry our clothes again. (5 hours from Dalwhinnie).

DAY FIVE.

Friday was once more dull and misty with intermittent showers but with the promise from the Met. Office of improvement. Skis were carried for about two kilometres above the Lodge until the river was crossed. Thereafter progress was on ski through the mist to the foot of the Long Leachas. When the angle became too steep, crampons and axe substituted for skis. The Long Leachas is a most attractive ridge and one of the finest approaches to Ben Alder. With four inches of new snow on top of old and with skis on frame rucksacks the ascent was not without difficulty. However, it was snowing gently and there was thick mist which reduced the feeling of exposure. Once on the plateau, the equipment change was reversed and a careful altimeter setting made. The two kilometres to the summit of Ben Alder were navigated painstakingly—mindful of the heavily corniced edge of the Garbh Choire. For a moment at the cairn, the sun seemed about to shine. Then all was white again. Total white-out, giving rise to acute vertiginous sensations on the descent, due to the complete lack of sensory stimuli. A simple bearing led on to the great west ridge of Ben Alder on splendid snow and the mist cleared at about 900 metres allowing a more rapid and relaxed run down to the Bealach Cumhann. After lunch on the Bealach, the descent was resumed. The Uisge Labhair was crossed easily on foot and a jigsaw of interconnecting snow patches ran into a long snow-filled gully which gave an excellent descent to the bridge at Corrour Shooting Lodge. (7 hours from Culra Lodge). A food cache was collected from the keeper there and he very obligingly gave us the use of a ghillies' bothy for the night. (The planned overnight stop was Ben Alder Cottage, on a west-east traverse). The arrival from Glasgow of Sandy Cousins an hour later was an unexpected but welcome surprise. He acted as hut custodian and general guardian angel for the next 36 hours.

DAY SIX.

Saturday was a clear day with a powdering of new snow on the ground and a bitterly cold north-west wind. It was possible to put skis on at the side of the road and follow the edge of the plantation to the Allt Loch na Lap and thence westwards on to the ridge of Beinn na Lap in the lee of which a well marked windslab was forming. On the summit the cold was very severe with considerable spindrift. Westward, the Mamores and our ultimate goal of Nevis looked magnificent. Conditions for the descent were the best yet— soft powder on a frozen base, extending right down to the Loch Treig railway line. The walk round the head of Loch Treig and up the glen to Staoineag Bothy was quite springlike in the warm afternoon sun, a strange contrast to conditions on the mountain. Nor was there anything springlike about the icy waters of the Amhainn Rath which we had to wade to reach the bothy. (7½ hours from Corrour Lodge). Staoineag was another five-star bothy. Sandy Cousins in his *gardien* role had preceded us and superintended an excellent dinner which was consumed in front of a crackling fire.

DAY SEVEN.

Reveille was 04.00 hrs. An hour later, by torchlight, the river crossing was reversed—no easy task as the stepping stones were glazed with ice and the banks white with frost. Torchlight was necessary as far as Luibeilt. The snowline was reached shortly after a memorable dawn and we donned Harscheisen to give a grip in the hard frozen crust. The line of a stream took us to the shoulder of Sgùrr Choinnich Mór, which was followed steeply to just below the summit, the last fifty metres being done on foot on account of a slightly unstable wind slab. The scene was superb, a day in a hundred; snow peaks on all sides, sharp ridges, steep rocky corries and over all, a deep blue sky.

A long descending traverse on good snow, skirting the shoulder of Sgùrr Choinnich Beag, led easily to the col below the great Buttress of Aonach Beag. This was turned on the left by ascending delicately to the Sgùrr a Bhuic col using crampons. From the col, a long gradual ski ascent led up to the ridge of Aonach Beag and the summit at 12.45 hrs. The run down to the Aonach Dubh col was quick and enjoyable. However the slope leading over to the Carn Mór Dearg col was unskiable. This was disappointing as we had both successfully skied the slope the previous May. In fact, it was quite poisonous, with soft new snow lying on old, and numerous patches of green ice. Not only were axe and crampons required, but the rope was brought into use on the steepest part of the slope. A lot of precious time was lost in reaching the col and as a result lunch was delayed till 14.30 hrs. This unfortunately led to a flagging of energy and spirits on the ascent of Carn Mór Dearg and the day came close to being abandoned on that summit at 16.00 hrs. However strength and reserve returned at the brave sight of Nevis in the late afternoon sun. A few parties were still at work in the gullies. The weather remained very settled and a slight wind had dropped again. Needless to say we carried our skis over the Carn Mór Dearg arête. It was in excellent condition with a generous covering of firm snow and forty minutes sufficed to reach the final slope of Nevis, the summit being attained at 17.20 hrs. as the sun set. No other human was in sight as the water bottles were drained and the last chocolate bar consumed.

The descent from Nevis in the grey light of evening was a fitting climax to the trip. Five hundred metres of perfect powder was followed by a further four hundred metres of variable packed snow, frozen crust and Easter snow. Ski-ing petered out at the bend on the tourist path below Lochan Meall an t'Suidhe. As darkness fell, we strapped our skis on our rucksacks for the last time and began the painfully laborious descent. The final mud slide to the Youth Hostel in Glen Nevis was accomplished by torchlight, arriving at 19.30 hrs. on Sunday night. (14 hrs. from Staoineag Bothy).

This completed a hundred miles of ski-ing across the Scottish Highlands, and a most enjoyable and eventful week's holiday. The car was retrieved from the car park in Fort William, but unable to obtain an evening meal in Lochaber we had to keep the hunger pangs at bay until the chip shop in Kingussie. The Grieve caravan was used for a brief overnight stop before driving back to Aberdeen and Peterhead in time for Monday morning surgeries.

CONCLUSIONS.

The map (page 229) gives a diagramatic representation of the Scottish Haute Route and compares it with the classic Haute Route from Chamonix to Zermatt. It will be seen that the distances involved are generally greater in Scotland but the altitude differences are broadly comparable. The effects of altitude in the Alps are offset by heavier rucksacks in Scotland. A fundamental difference between the two routes is that the Alpine Haute Route generally follows the line of least resistance through cols whereas the Scottish route crosses the mountain tops which is aesthetically more satisfying. Having done the Verbier variant of the Alpine route the previous year, we were agreed that the Scottish route was the more demanding physically and at least as hard in technical terms. Objective dangers are undoubtedly greater in the Alps. However, recent accidents in Scottish hills have demonstrated once again that avalanche hazards must not be underestimated and that it is all too easy to ski over a cornice in a whiteout.

One decided advantage of Scotland which has a special appeal to the Aberdonian character is cost. There are no hut charges in Scottish bothies and the party had its cheapest holiday in years.

THE THIN MAN AND TWO RUCKSACKS

By David Snadden

I LEFT the road in the company of my wife and Derwent Turnbull, with Derwent's three dogs bounding energetically along in front. We were heading up the Coire Dubh path between Beinn Eighe and Liathach, the morning light making the slopes of Beinn Eighe seem much gentler than they really are, a fact we soon discovered when we left the path and started the gruesome haul up to the ridge. Moira and the dogs were soon mere specks on the skyline. Much sweating and one or two scenery stops saw Derwent and myself arriving on the ridge to find her reclining in the sun amidst a heap of tangled dogs. After a much needed rest we set off in the direction of Ruadh-Stac Mór, leaving the col between it and A'Choinneach Mhór to contour round to Coire Ruadh-Staca. The two and a half hours there certainly seemed the quickest, if most masochistic, way.

As we made our way round the vague path into the corrie we were suddenly confronted with a jumble of rock towers, seeming acres of quartzite which are difficult to see from virtually anywhere on Beinn Eighe except, perhaps, Ruadh-Stac-Beag.

'That's the best route in the corrie,' said Derwent, pointing to the right hand of two obvious ridges. This was first climbed in 1971 by D. Howard, C. S. Rose and R. W. L. Turnbull and christened Thin Man's Ridge for reasons which will soon become apparent.

I tipped the contents of my sack on to the ground and, after a slight diversion to rescue Moira's rucksack, which had gone for a merry jaunt down the mountainside, roped up to her. Derwent disappeared into the gully on our left followed by his still energetic dogs.

The first pitch started with a short wall which led to a man-sized chimney surmounted by a precarious chockstone, this providing an energetic thrutch on to a good ledge. Moira followed amid much cursing as she managed to get herself plus rucksack jammed in the chimney, so that she was facing the wrong way to even see the vital hold. A judicious heave on the sack and all was well. A short easy pitch led to the first terrace, where Derwent was standing camera in hand. Escape from this point is relatively easy.

Above us loomed an impressive tower, its right hand side split by a large cleft, capped by a large overhang. The narrowness of the cleft compelled me to leave my rucksack behind, in the hope that there might be enough rope to haul it from the top of the tower. The way into the cleft proved awkward, an insecure move over an airy gap to the welcoming embrace of cold stone walls, which disappeared into the murky depths of the tower. Some twenty feet inside the cleft the way was blocked by loose boulders, a gentle push sent these crashing into the depths of the mountainside. The way now being clear I carried on along the narrow dark passage, flickering rays of light guiding me out into a small airy cave. Below, Allt Coire Ruadh-Staca meandered gently to Loch Maree, the scene breathtakingly enhanced by menacing dark clouds boiling over Slioch and obscuring the remote peaks of Letterewe. Though the cave was the obvious belay point, thoughts of marooned rucksacks caused me to climb on to the top of the tower, no easy matter with appalling rope drag trying to pluck me off fortunately good holds. Needless to say, once at the top there was not enough rope.

Moira eventually understood that my garbled shouts meant that she would have to climb with both sacks. The rope came on for a bit, then stopped for an indeterminable length of time, its immobility accompanied by high pitched subterranean squeals which were wafting out of the mouth of the cave. At this time she was having a private epic, the ground below was awfully far away, the rucksacks, penduluming from her shoulders on long straps, were threatening to pull her from her meagre balance holds, and, to crown all, the slack hadn't been taken in completely. The rope tightened and she got over the awkward move into the cleft. At least her legs did; wedged there by her dumpy feet, her torso hanging over nothing, she struggled out of the sacks and thrutched, one handed, into the safety of the cleft, hanging desperately to the sacks with her trailing arm. As this limb weakened the squeals grew more anguished at the thought of corrie-bound belongings, until, in a flash of inspiration, she put her vocal strength into her failing muscles and the sacks arrived beside her. A few moments later she arrived beside me, hot, sweaty and somewhat less than amiable.

The way now led to a small grassy bay from which an amphitheatre of rock sprang. To the right, separated from this by a gully, rose an impressive tower, even more imposing than the first. The route went up the right hand side of this, on the edge of a face dropping steeply to the screes several hundred feet below. A gloriously exposed pitch on sound, compact quartzite led to a large detached pinnacle perched high on the side of the tower. At the base of this a small platform provided a very exposed stance. Not far above was the top of the tower, inaccessible behind a line of overhangs, with to the right, a steep blank wall falling to the screes below. The vista of Loch Maree and the now emergent peaks of Letterewe was available to any eye not too engrossed in where to go next. A line of scant footholds disappeared round the corner, above them the overhangs, below, a long way it seemed, the top of the first tower. For the first few feet there were handholds of sorts, these petered out leaving only balance and the lure of a big foothold peeping out from around the corner. A long stretch over nothing, then the security of jumbled blocks and the drop quickly diminishing from its previous hundreds of feet. I had at least revelled in the knowledge that the route went that way, a fact that only increases admiration for the first ascentionists.

Moira again excelled here, the final stretch being too much for her wee legs, she made a spectacular leap across fresh air to the safety of the blocks, this somewhat unorthodox ploy surprising her out-of-sight leader, the warning shout having been carried away by the strong breeze.

A hundred feet of Alpine-like scrambling on a sharp arête of solid blocks terminated in a short wall and a hairy welcome from

Derwent's dogs. The way back was to the main ridge and then down the knee-punishing slopes to the road, the not so energetic dogs walking to heel unbidden, Moira a speck in the distance—behind this time, having got mildly off course on the way down.

Next time the rucksacks will stay at the bottom.

A GRAND DAY ON THE GRAN PARADISO

By Clive Laviolette

In Vol. XXXI of the *Journal*, amongst the reports of the Activities of the S.M.C. and J.M.C.S. abroad, under the general heading of 'The Alps,' appears the following terse statement:

'We drove round for the *voie normale* on the Gran Paradiso . . . . This was a long easy plod from the Victor Emmanuel hut, made notable by perfect visibility round the compass . . . .'

The full story behind this bald account opens towards late evening on a road in a wet, mist-draped valley near Zinal in Switzerland. Our elderly Volkswagen camping van grinds protestingly upwards. My wife eyes the damp hills which are to be her home for the next fourteen days with distaste, and the coil-spring bends of the road, her escape route to the civilisation of the Rhone Valley below, with horror. This is not what she has been promised! Where are those sun-drenched Alps of last year so vividly described to her? Surely we have taken a wrong turning and are in reality climbing the Bealach Na Ba to endure yet another wet holiday in the West? But no, the road's end shows us that this is indeed the place. Look at all those brave, wet, familiar faces peering out of the gathering darkness!

After greetings are exchanged the grisly tale unfolds: nothing but rain for five days, nothing climbed, prices as high as the mountains, spirits as low as the cloud level. However, if the weather changes a nice little jaunt has been planned. Nothing drastic, just a 'wee jog' up to a high hut and then an easy top within staggering distance. A mental orchestra in my brain strikes up 'on with the motley, the paint and the powder.' I make noises designed to express neither interest nor reluctance. After all, these two heroes in front of me are not merely friends. They are the reason why I, a youthful ingenue of some forty brief summers, am now in the J.M.C.S. They are my alpha and omega. They are my Proposer and Seconder. To let them down would be unthinkable. Anyway, maybe it will rain for another five days. It does!

The scene shifts to sunny Val d'Aosta. In Italy all is brightness, warmth and light. The mountains stand around benevolent warm, and beckoning. With our crossing of the Gran S. Bernardino the grim past fades with the mist. Suddenly we are all Italian. *Gracies, pregos* and *chaios* roll fluently from the lips. The Seconder admits he has always had his eye on the Gran Paradiso. A 'wee jog' up to the hut and then an easy dawdle to the top the next day. Readers will recognise the reappearance of that old refrain. It's a tune which seems to form the leit-motif of many hill days.

Leaving no time for second thoughts, that afternoon finds our three heroes in the valley of Valsavranche, hot-footing it along the path towards the Rifugio Vittorio Emmanuele. The drive up the valley is a memorable experience. Mountain villages, beautifully balanced in their random location, not yet renovated or modernised. Tiny churches with hardly room to swing a censer. A gloriously plunging river, pine trees, the valley becoming more wild and beautiful at every turn, until the road ends in a setting of mountain perfection. To make an odious comparison, it all looks just as the Lost Valley of Glencoe might have done a million or so years ago, if you ignore the Albergo in the right-hand corner. The path to the hut is a minor work of art in its engineering, situation and routeing. At the top, fifty yards off, ibex stare at us with mild annoyance but no fear. When we pass they drop down to the path behind and descend to the valley. A great eye for an easy line seems common to man and beast in this part of Italy.

Sunset finds our three grand lads slipping into their sacks in the old refuge building. Purists have described this older building as being more in keeping with the surroundings, but we choose to sleep in it less for an aesthetic principle than because it is cheaper. The night is spent tossing about on hard hut beds, you know the sort, as we try vainly to snatch even an hour's sleep.

At last day breaks. The Seconder, a lad light in years but heavy in experience, says it is no good pushing off in the dark and stumbling through the boulder fields. A wait of thirty minutes will give enough light to save our energy and pick our way without torches.

The Proposer is all for a quick start. Why delay when he can see his way clearly to the top? He proves his point half-an-hour later by demonstrating that you can stumble through boulders even in broad daylight. Ahead of us up the snowfields winds the long line of early risers who have stumbled through the boulders, wasted their torch batteries and their energies, and are now easily passed by us.

At this point in the narrative the casual reader, and aren't we all, will have noticed that although we have had action, setting, characters, music and plot, there has been precious little dialogue.

Of course we did bandy a few words, but it has been my experience that what is funny at 1,000 ft., hilarious at 5,000 ft., and rib-busting at 12,000 ft. sounds very thin at sea level, and reads even more so. In my view, mountain dialogue tends to be disparaging, vulgar and rude, an opinion which will be confirmed before our story ends.

We plod on. Suddenly our New Member's positive thinking, which has got him up to 11,000 ft., turns sour on him. He is now only positive that he cannot get up the last 1,000 ft. To hell with what his two sponsors think. There is just not enough strength left in his legs. His heart pounds, his breath comes in short pants. After a rest, the cold drains away the last of his resolution. His suggestion that the party leave him behind is utterly rejected by the senior member, who takes his pack. The Seconder, equally constructive, suggests 'wee steps.' In his foolishness the New Member saw 'wee steps' merely as long steps shortened. But believe me, 'wee steps' worked for him, and they can work for you too. The theory behind them, as the Seconder explained, is this. The man in front takes such small steps that the hitherto lagging second man is dogging his footsteps. Eventually the laggard feels the man in front is in the way. He wants to get past, to assert his superior speed. We 'wee stepped' our way upwards!

The summit, with a cast of thousands. The sun is shining, not a cloud in the sky, every mountain for a hundred miles is clearly visible. The Proposer and Seconder shake your hand. You have climbed your first 4,000 m. Alpine peak. You have justified their faith in you, and it's your turn to buy the drinks below. My mental orchestra swells to a crescendo with a heady mixture of 'Thus Spake Zarathustra,' 'Hymn of Joy,' and 'Mass for a Thousand Voices.' I count off the peaks, starting with Monte Leone in Italy, La Meije and Les Ecrins in France, the whole of the Mont Blanc range, the Matterhorn, the Dom, the Monch, etc., etc., etc. I know someone will write in to say you cannot see all these peaks from Gran Paradiso, but he wasn't there that day and I was. Neither of my two mentors in their combined Alpine experience have ever seen such a view. You are, they both assure you, a lucky wee lad.

We descend easily, surfeited with peaks, in long strides. Gaily down the snow slopes so painfully gained, past the hut and down the path to the valley bottom we flash. Passing a delightful signorina in the act of removing her skirt to sun-bathe, I miss my footing. My Proposer speaks the only recorded dialogue of this great day:

'I'm surprised at you! She's old enough to be your wife!'

THE PIG

By John Mackenzie

TOM HAS the answer, he has been there before, all the way up Glen F. but not quite, then right by the path and into the Pigs' Hole*. 'Yes, there are lines.' Two he thinks, but then it was from the Sea Pink's summit after all and distance does not lend to clarity. A rummage through District Guides is equally disparaging, vegetable and of little account, which means in 1933 they probably got a fright. It is worth a look after all.

So I phone up Ma Kettle; she is very nice and gives us a permit. We turn left after the bridge and stop at the gate. It is no ordinary gate this, but one with padlocks. Twelve in all, seven for the days in the week and the rest for holidays. In between, the links peer shyly out at us, too narrow to file, so we get the key from the house on the left. Up we go, a good but winding road over hills with corners and small bridges with z-bends. The scenery grows wilder, the hills white and then the mist drops down. Still we go on up this interminable track until just past the concrete bridge. It is cold enough and we walk up the path. Again, like the gate, no ordinary path, for an R.A.F. Land Rover appears from behind, passing us, with beery faces pressed close to the windows. Their victory is short lived however, they have come to a halt a mere 200 yards further. But have they too heard of the Pigs' Hole? Spurred, the strides lengthen, they recede into the distance and we do not see them again. On our right the river plunges over falls and runs throatily through hidden depths, so we follow on for a further mile straining against the obscuring mist.

Suddenly it is there, the great headland of the Pig, it looks huge but then the mist closes in as we skirt her base, seeing starts but no finishes. The loch is on our left now and the corrie arches round. Tom points up and beyond: I see grey mist, snow and black rock, impossible to assess or dismiss. We go on for another upward mile and as we approach the Sea Pink's south summit, her eastern face bristles with lines. Huge corners and grooves dissolve and reform in the grey film; all so steep and uncertain that we must rub noses before the secrets are no more.

A long diagonal slant runs beneath her face, bottomed by short sections of glass, over which we approach. The largest corner is some way up, white but terribly steep with a traverse beckoning to

---

*Readers who wish to clarify the obscure geography and nomenclature of this article are referred to p. 280.

Photo: Des Marshall

The South Peak of the Cobbler from the Central Peak. *Climber, Keith Burns*

August, 1976

Photo: W. D. Brooker

Squareface in the Garbh Choire of Beinn a Bhuird—
the finish is by the prominent crack(S) or the line just to its right (V.D.)

its foot. So left we go, ever steepening, into the gully. Perfect it is too, with old grey water ice and nevé leading to the start of the corner. It is like looking at Unicorn, rock with an inch of powder snow somehow resting, but on the right is our escape, a long slanting rake going across the wall, hidden at the top by a twist. On the left a saddle gives perfect belays. We rope and munch and exchange gear. I go down, then up again to gain our line and nevé and ice lead ever upward to a secure tether at rope's end. Tom flails past like an old thresher and recedes into the mist. There is a shout and a powder woofer flies by, followed by another, and another. They are at least regular, ten minutes on the dot, so I join Tom in five and step out right to get one in the face. The angle steepens and the cornice is complete and inescapable. Mini woofers slide over the top and down out of my breeches. Unconsolidated snow arches out as quickly as I smash it down, until with effort an exit is made into a regular maelstrom onto the plateau.

We stagger off down the other side. It is long and arduous and we are very wet when we reach the lodge by the loch. My back and his knee both hurt so we lurch along the road and past the dam like a pair of cripples. The dam is arcuate and a fine effort, well worth admiring, but my back still hurts and his knee is worse, so the final mile is slow. One route does not a crag make, so we must return.

The blizzards came shortly after and the resurrection of sheep took the place of the white slopes, but the lure of the Pig eventually called us again.

Rucksack and I, old friends, took the car to the gate in snow far whiter and deeper than before. The odd flake still floated down and the clouds gave a hint of future menace. Deep ruts lined the road so we swung wildly on the straight, slewed on corners and spun on the hills. A feature of this glen is that the hills slope down when going up and up when going down, so I spun, slewed and swung all the way to the little concrete bridge, now nearly buried in snow. Deer line the path, hinds and stags grouping in hungry herds, muzzles unable to pierce the frozen desert; we feel for them but know that hay bales will be given later. Now the track has disappeared and is replaced by a bank of nevé sloping ever steeply into the now silent burn. Crampons traverse slopes where before we had scampered. Still the flakes fall, the cloud becomes ragged, heavier and tinged with purple. Plagued with doubt we head on, under the Pig and across the frozen loch to take a seat roughly at its centre. The mist lifts, so levering the frozen rear off the ice, we step more lightly up to Sea Pink.

We decide we shall start gently, considering Rucksack's inability to stay put and his fondness for gravity. Tying him on I head for the long corner on the edge of the face, up perfect nevé and rapidly mounting peer occasionally down to see how he is faring. All is well and two rope lengths to an impasse go quickly. Ahead is no use, far too steep and thin, so right it is, up a nice groove then back left by some ice to a broad easy snow fan. Rucksack climbs well; never one to follow the easiest line, he bounces happily over futuristic problems to re-unite us before the little cornice.

On the crest we walk north to the farthest and least corniced exit of the slanting gully and descend steeply below the face to espy the groove. This is uphill from Tom's line and looking anxiously at Rucksack I dig him a good stance. Now the groove is long and steep and filled entirely with water ice but with a wall on the left and icy slabs on the right. Resting against the wall, I look down every now and again giving him a wary glance. The ice is very thin and keeps breaking off, but improves above until a small saddle on the right gives me a chance to bring him up. Crossing a bay a steepening groove topped by an icy bulge stops all progress. Somewhat pounded in a cramped bridge beneath it, I alert a somnolent and apathetic Rucksack before addressing the problem. A contorted move right produces two firm placements over the bulge and with much scratching and scraping I emerge clear above amidst a welter of icicles, which tinkle down the groove and beyond, their musical chatter growing ever more distant. Above, a horrendous cornice blocks all exit, about thirty feet high and double, topping a widening and steepening groove. I excavate Rucksack an extra secure stance.

'You do not belong here,' I tell the cornice. 'You belong on the Ben,' but the twin-headed monster merely leers drunkenly forward, an idiot giant. On the right a shallow tunnel curves into him, so I have a look, clearing away the powder until firmer snow is reached. But the angle rears up through thirty degrees and a few feet from the eave I come to a full stop. All in a dither, I return to the stance for a re-think. Over to the left is a shallow scoop leading to an icy slope where the overhang is smaller. So smiling wanly at Rucksack this line is followed to a crouched stance. An icy blast hurls stinging needles of spindrift which soon accumulate to form a frozen mask. Ice encrusted vision forces a quick solution, so threshings and excavation reduce the cornice edge until an icy, incoherently mumbling figure rolls over onto the plateau.

Rucksack follows splendidly but then spoils it all by sticking himself awkwardly under the lip. A sinking resignation settles, only to be released by a sudden serendipity when he unexpectedly leaps over the top. Hidden by mist before, the col between the peaks is soon reached and we descend quickly to the loch.

Back in the car some snow had fallen and the ominous clouds have retreated to a point halfway down the glen where they sit in obstinate splendour. All goes well for the first few miles, the fresh stuff is only inches deep and the way quite clear. Stopping to take photos of roadside stags, we trundle happily along the glen, at least as far as the cloud wall. Entering this different world light flees, snow falls thick and heavily whilst the road plays hide and seek with the banks. It now more closely resembles the path to some frozen Hades and incipient panic becomes a heated grapple with the steering wheel. Here the road is a series of hills going up, all with wicked bends, so we go fast, but then too fast, as the corner swings hard away from the crest. We skid first left then right to regain a semblance of control at one of the many bridges, to see just ahead in the murk faint tail lights. It is an estate Land Rover on its way back after feeding the deer.

I chortle merrily, it is so easy following the tracks, but then he stops and on a hill. Instant panic, for I cannot start as he pulls away again. Damn all false hopes, but I start in third and catch up. He stops, but this time to the side to let me by; such kindness leads to no good and the car recommences its rake's progress. At long last the gate with many locks appears and we stop inches away. On the main road much has fallen and I call at Ma Kettle's leaving snow on her carpet, but being furtive, place it back in my pocket.

Up the long glen past abandoned cars, until the Myrtle bridge is reached. Beyond, is a long ascending hill complete with corner, so very cautiously in fourth we head round; but no, too fast, the vehicle slews on hidden ice and takes the corner sideways, a correction and we are all okay but gibbering, so it is ultra cautious to home.

Next weekend the sun bursts from a cloudless blue and we head for the Pig once more, but this time there are no epics, just good days with bruised knuckles on hard ice and piercing cold, Jerry, Tom, Rucksack and I wallowing in it, and wanting more.

A SENSE OF BELONGING

Most at ease among the mountains
For they tell of youth and mystery—
And all men would travel backwards:
The womb is warm!
            Did you smell the sea?
Did you lie in heather with diamonds overhead?
Or see all secrets in a snowflake?
Did you weep for joy and, in the morning place,
All hungers fill and fearful thirst slake?

HAMISH M. BROWN.

WANDERLUST

By Ted Maden

I STOMPED up the path in black mood. My three companions were lost to sight, having raced ahead like greyhounds. I prepared to weather the scathing comments on the subject of my general unfitness, which my straggling arrival at the lochan would undoubtedly occasion.

'Hullo, Ted. Fine morning. Take a good rest. Have some chocolate.'

Ken's mild mannered greeting came as such a pleasant surprise that I failed completely to consider its possible portent. I, too, in a climbing career punctuated by moments of enterprise, have been meticulously polite to unsuspecting seconds for whom a day of truth lay ahead.

The Post Face of Meagaidh stood full into the March morning sun, but around the corner the Inner Corrie was in shadow and promised to retain the overnight frost. Ian and C.D. had already appraised this situation and were heading straight towards the Pumpkin. This caused Ken some slight momentary discomfiture, but further to the right the Diadem cut a fine line through the upper cliffs. That would do. We were to escape with a IV.

The Diadem starts up a moderate-angled snow gully which leads into a central snow fan, whence a steep snow and ice gully slices through the upper cliffs to the summit cornice. Well to the left of this upper, central gully an even steeper line of snow and ice bulges lent atmosphere to the surroundings, though this fact may only be of mild scenic interest.

We put on crampons and walked round a frozen avalanche cone to the start of the initial gully. In the gully Ken paused from time to time, and I would suppose that he was seeking a stance at which to rope up. Actually he was just having a blow and a grin and a peek at the view. We continued thus for some height before I realized that the intention was to solo all the way to the start of the principal difficulties. Just below the top of the gully the angle steepened, and a glance downwards to the knobbly avalanche cone indicated that the time had come not to trip over my crampons. Ken had by now surmounted the central snowslope and was searching for a belay at the foot of the upper rocks. I followed to a point where the snowslope was intersected by a short band of mixed rock and ice. The drop below was now lethal and a hitherto vague thought crystallized in my mind: I was gripped. I cut an enormous step, dug in my claws and terrordactyls and demanded a top rope. After much hammering of belay pins Ken unwound his 50 metres of perlon and lowered an end, which I was just able to reach. The rock was awkward enough to make me glad that no notions of foolish pride had inhibited me from requesting the rope.

I noticed something odd about Ken's stance. It was not located on the direct line of Diadem, but well to the left, below the other line of very steep ice bulges in fact. He informed me that these had been climbed, that the climb was called the Wand and that it looked interesting. It went smack up a formidable inside corner formed by the intersection between four consecutive ice bulges on the left and a slightly impending rock wall on the right. At a guess there were a hundred and twenty feet of very hard climbing before the angle eased. The stance was already exposed, our separation from the Diadem was by a sixty degree headwall of snow and rock, and any thought that I may have entertained of sneaking furtively back down into the corrie was rendered impracticable by my absolute requirement for Ken's co-operation with the rope. He remained impeccably polite over small details, chatting amiably and offering me lunch, which congealed in my mouth. We tied on to the second rope and draped ourselves with equipment. There remained just one small point. It might get steep ahead; Ken would leave his rucksack at the stance.

Moving up the few feet of easy-angled snow to the first bulge, it immediately became apparent that the surface material consisted not of good snow-ice but of some inches of rotten, scaly snow, which had decayed during a recent thaw and had then re-frozen. Front pointing was out of the question. Ken had to clear away the rotten stuff and cut steps in the underlying water-ice. From below, the first bulge did not look as steep as the upper ones, yet even here progress was extremely slow. Every move had to be planned and cut in advance. The right wall hereabouts was festooned with massive icicles, so that it was not possible to place a rock peg for protection. Moreover the icicles extended to directly above my head, and gave me a good deal of concern lest the frost should lose its grip. For all of these reasons I hoped that Ken would be sensible, realize the impossibility of his task and quit early. Instead he progressed, slowly but steadily, until at twenty-five feet he was able to place a good ice screw. Soon afterwards he had surmounted the first steep section and had reached a resting point in the corner. Another bulge, climbed with much one-handed step-cutting, led to a constricted resting point some sixty feet up, between the impending rock wall and the steepest of the ice bulges.

The next ten feet appeared crucial. He placed a good rock peg but for some time thereafter it seemed doubtful from below whether any real progress was being made at all. Repeated bouts of one-handed cutting were followed by retreats for rests, and sometimes two or three sorties yielded only a single new step.

'How does it compare with Vanishing?'

'Far harder.'

Not very encouraging. I sheltered under the protective canopy of icicles from the intermittent hail of cuttings. During the intervals between Ken's sorties I gazed out from my eyrie, down slopes which looked much steeper from above than from below, into the corrie where a few tiny figures passed and were gone, up the opposite hillside, covered with scree and snow, where a person might move freely, and at the sky which I studied intently for signs of changing weather. Fortunately this seemed to be fairly stable. Occasionally a breeze would cause me to shiver. When it died down the shivering would cease. Simple heat exchange. As a further diversion I had been photographing Ken's progress. This involved leaning on the belay ropes far out from under the protecting icicles, whilst simultaneously craning upwards through the viewfinder, fumbling with the shutter control and trying to retain a grip of the climbing ropes. The operation was so exquisitely delicate that it provided total if temporary relief from the tension of the climb.

'Make sure you hold that rope!'

The word, 'rope,' was preceded by a forceful adjective. I gathered Ken was about to make The Move. He climbed with control and precision up his precut steps, over the bulge, and was soon cutting a small resting platform above the crux. Optimism now rang in his voice. He placed another runner, cut a few more steps in a final bulge and was soon out of sight. And earshot. The ropes continued to run out. The thick 150 ft. rope went tight. I gathered from vague shouts that he was almost there. I untied the thick rope. The end snaked up to the first bulge. The thin 50 metre rope went tight. Was he belayed? Communication was impossible. I would have to prepare to climb.

Still belayed, I stuffed Ken's not quite empty rucksack into my not quite empty one to produce a far from empty package that was by no means light, and about as bulky and unwieldy as a suitcase. Next I adjusted my items of equipment. Then, deciding that the thin rope had been tight for long enough to warrant positive action, I hammered out the two belay pegs, played a final jingle on the hardware and started to climb.

After mounting the ten feet of easy-angled snow I paused at the foot of the first bulge to give Ken time to belay, in case by any chance he should not already have done so. I had also planned at this point to tie on to the end of the thick rope, but this was now half way up the first bulge. I started up the bulge in pursuit. After just two moves I appreciated Ken's problem. As already mentioned, he had had to cut steps into good ice some inches below the poor surface snow. The angle was such that 'below' meant inwards. Thus on standing in the steps I found my nose pressed against the snow.

It might seem that all that was required was to keep it there and continue climbing up Ken's steps. This was easier said than done, however, and after ten feet I knew that I was in difficulties. In my right hand was a good Terrordactyl. In my other hand was a larger McInnes axe whose pick was mounted at a less acute angle than the beak of a true 'Terror.' All winter I had been intending to have this angle changed, but I had not got round to it, an oversight which I now deeply regretted. The suitcase-like rucksack was pulling me off backwards, my right arm, clinging to the one good 'Terror,' was tiring rapidly and I still had not caught up with the thick rope. A slip would have sent me yo-yoing down to the bottom of the pitch where I would be held if the thin rope did not cut under tension. The whole thing gave me the heebee-jeebees.

'I can't do it. The rucksack's pulling me off backwards and the 'Terror' won't hold.'

Ken's reply wafted faintly down from an incredible height.

'It's . . . All . . . In . . . The . . . Mind.'

Remote, but typical Crocket. Pull yourself together, Maden. I learnt subsequently that he had not heard the bit about the Terrordactyl.

It was impossible to rely on the longer axe when held in the conventional manner, with the hand on the shaft and the sling around the wrist for weight-bearing. I therefore curled my fingers round the head of this axe, thus minimizing any outward pull, and rammed it in by pick or adze until it seemed that it might momentarily hold. Then, my heart in my mouth, I extracted the good 'Terror,' jabbed it in higher, felt it tear sickeningly downwards, jabbed again, hoped that one or other implement would grip while I moved a foot up into the next step, and shouted:

'Up rope!'

After three or four such appallingly precarious and staccato moves I reached and grasped the sling which hung from Ken's ice-screw. I used this to the full for progress and resting. Around here I also caught up with the thick rope, tied on, and began to feel marginally more secure. I even managed to remove the ice-screw A few more steep moves brought me to the first niche, which provided a surprisingly comfortable stance.

Ahead, in two sections, rose the inside corner on which Ken had spent so much time. The average angle was almost vertical and the situation was so exposed as to seem more like a rock climb than an ice climb. A rock climb! Why not? I shoved my back and the offending suitcase against the rock wall, kicked my crampons at Ken's steps and flailed the 'Terrors' at anything in sight. And so I progressed inelegantly to the second niche. I noted that Ken's good rock peg was indeed good. The crux bulge reared ahead. I wondered whether the brute force tactics which had served me thus far would succeed on this daunting obstacle. At least the thick rope now provided tangible support and we were communicando again. Nevertheless, I shall not dwell on the details of my crux dash. Suffice it to say that my climbing was a desperate thrutch on ice, and achieved only the bare essential of delivering me, gasping, over the bulge.

The exit from the top of the corner was via a short, steep section of ice on the left wall. Ken had disposed of this with relative ease before disappearing from view. However I was not yet out of the wood. I unclipped a final runner, and the ropes then ran up left and out of sight. A miscalculation might well lead to a pendule out of the corner and across the face. Fortunately I did not pendule but eventually emerged on to a 'gentle' slope of no more than fifty degrees. I was forty feet diagonally below Ken on terrain which, even now, was serious: rubbishy snow on ice, in which Ken had still found sufficient energy to cut good steps. I moved thankfully up these until for the last few feet the angle steepened again. Surely I would not normally find such a short section so utterly exhausting. I was shattered.

A hundred and sixty feet; two hours each. We learnt subsequently that Lang and Quinn had split the pitch into three or four shorter pitches on the first ascent. Meanwhile Ken sat shivering in a little rock cave belayed to a chockstone in a crack in the roof. As I had suspected, the finishing touches to this belay had been engineered after my departure from the stance at the foot of the pitch.

The cloud was now down and it was not obvious which way was out. My leader correctly perceived that his second was in no shape to take over the initiative in this respect. So we crawled around the cave and swopped positions and belays and gear, and Ken made a few steep moves up from the right hand end of the cave onto a snow ramp from which another bulge led into the unknown. However, the snow ramp also continued to the right, and with the rigours of the summit plateau still to contend with the time did not seem ripe for direct finishes. So he led, and eventually I followed, away to the right and into the summit couloir of Diadem. A mildly insecure finish to the right of the big cornice brought us out onto the misty summit plateau.

Crampon tracks led rightwards to where, somewhere, we must descend to the Window. It was vital not to descend too soon or we would become ensnared by the last climbs in the corrie. The tracks parted, some descending to the right. Too soon? We followed the other tracks. They seemed to be going a long way round, and there were only two sets of them. As we later learnt, they had been made by Ian and C.D., who had finished the Pumpkin in mist only a short while before our emergence from our Wander. And so we floundered around the distant regions of Meagaidh for a while, and then stole up on the Window from behind and descended from the mist into the inner corrie.

I stumbled, last as usual, down the path and arrived after dusk. My companions had meanwhile decided upon the evening's activities: a quick pint at Roy Bridge before returning to Fersit to cook supper. But no team celebrates a couple of Grade V's with a single pint. After a few, my appetite, so delicate on the hill, returned with a vengeance. I unearthed from the depths of my rucksack some evil looking peanuts, which I gobbled up, and a hard boiled egg. The latter I raised and cracked against my skull. This caused great mirth in the convivial atmosphere that now reigned by the fireside in the bar, doubtless because of the illusion created that it was my head, not the egg, that cracked.

WEE MALKIE

By Raymond Simpson

ALAN and I found 'Wee Malkie' during a long summer spent walking and climbing in Kashmir. We had been travelling extremely light with a minimum of climbing equipment and few specific objectives during the early part of the summer which had been spent in the high valleys of Indian Kashmir on the borders of Ladakh. The five peaks we had enjoyed there more than satisfied us and when the monsoon winds began to blow we fled to the arid majesty of the Karakorum.

Here, the mountains overawed us with their gigantic scale and we were content to wander their flanks enjoying Hunza apricots. We had not, however, enjoyed the cliff-hanging truck ride up the Indus valley and resolved to return on foot by the old silk route across the ranges to the south of Nanga Parbat. After five days of tranquil walking we came to the first village of any size on the south side of the range. Some hours above this village, we were told, there lay an attractive lake surrounded by snow peaks. Intrigued, we stocked up with food and ascended by a cascading clear burn on a sandy track weaving up through old gnarled pines; dramatically changing in a few hours to grassy meadows framing a long blue glacial lake.

The vegetation here was green and lush, a welcome contrast to the high desert ranges where we had spent the last few weeks.

Masses of succulent yellow flowers tumbled to the shores of the lake on the surface of which was reflected a wall of snow peaks. 'High, but not too high' we thought, '19,000 feet at the most.' One dominated the others; its massive bell shaped summit, embellished with graceful flutings of snow, focussed our eyes and aspirations.

We pitched our tent on a flower-strewn bank facing the big peak A tantalising line led through a hanging glacier, skirting a steep rock band on the right and looked as if it might take us to the summit icefield. We estimated 3,000 ft. of mixed climbing on most of which we should be able to move together, apart from perhaps part of the rock band. The icefield? Well, it looked like just another uniform slope of nevé of the type we had become used to ascending and descending without too much difficulty on other peaks.

We cast a not too critical eye over minimal climbing equipment and meagre supply of food. We agreed that at least we could 'have a look at it,' after all it was just another hill to climb with definable difficulties. Or was it? It hung above our idyllic campsite threatening the contentment of yesterday with its challenge, giving nothing away to furtive glances for reassurance. Its face was enigmatic, flattened by the evening light, and as the sunset colours glowed and faded our hopes rose and fell as we peered into the shadows gathering across its enormous western front.

Some Gujar children were herding goats down by the lake, and when they collected round the door of the tent we asked them what they called the mountains. Their name for the big one transliterated into something like 'Wee Malkie' and for us this became its title.

A long day was spent mainly in a maze of little buttresses below the hanging glacier which we hoped would provide a route to the summit ice field. The lake grew smaller and smaller beneath our heels and it was with great relief that we threw the sacks down on top of a buttress just below the glacier. There was not really room even for our tiny tent but we contrived to erect it astride the crest. This perch afforded us magnificent views of the jagged brown peaks to the south. The face above us looked like a giant liquorice allsort with its alternating bands of rock and ice. The setting sun caught the undersides of the low creeping flowers which spread their tendrils amongst the rocks, gilding their petals with a brief but lovely luminosity. When this faded, the sudden chill forced us to seek in vain the comfort of sleep on one of those fitful nights where tiredness and excitement battle for control of the consciousness. We were glad when the watch said it was time to brew up and be off.

A living sea of cloud filled the valleys below us, creeping in smoky wisps up the gullies. Rock peaks emerged from the sea to the south and west and were already turning pink with the first sun, instilling a sense of urgency as we fumbled with crampons.

The terminal icefall had looked ugly from below, however a hidden ramp in the ice provided a steep but secure passage and we were soon making our way up the hanging glacier to below the summit icefield. From the top of the glacier a shallow couloir offered a route but we were surprised to find that the ridge on its right was relatively easy. We unroped and delighted in climbing the warm slabby rock, chuckling to ourselves that this enigmatic black patch, seen from afar and obviously the key to the route, could not stop us now and was in fact providing us with an easy line through some incredible rock and ice scenery. To our left the face rose in one great rock step of a thousand feet over which avalanches spewed from the ridge above to the hanging glacier below; to our right a chaotic face of steep ice and seracs tumbled down from the summit.

The sun was already on the summit icefield when we arrived at its foot, small stones stotting down from the ridge to the left, but the centre seemed to be safe enough, at least for the time being. We still did not know how long it would take but as we had climbed almost three thousand feet from our campsite we reckoned that it could not be very much further.

Two hours later we were well beyond the point of no return but were still barely halfway up the icefield, having seriously under-estimated the length, steepness and hardness of the ice. Our situation was delicate; for five rope lengths we had been strung out on a slope of brittle water ice, our blunted crampons skating on the glassy surface. Because of a botched boot repair in Hunza, involving a chunk of tractor tyre, I could put no pressure on my front points and was forced into the strenuous contortions at which the French are said to excel. The brittle nature of the ice and the need for speed ruled out step cutting; even our drive in peg would not penetrate without fracturing the ice so that we could only belay the leader on each run out with our one tubular screw; the second following perforce with a tight rope on a psychological belay. Fortunately at mid-height the slope, being convex, eased slightly and we could traverse by means of frozen-in rocks to the relative security of a ridge where the snow cover was more generous. Thus for another eight rope lengths to the summit dome, where, gasping for breath in the thin air, we collapsed in the soft snow, ten hours from the tent.

By this time in the day the views to the north were obscured by cloud but we could see the lake far below, looking so incredibly small that it was hard to believe that this massive peak and all the others could ever have been mirrored in its tiny surface. We could not afford to hang about however as we were anxious to find a descent route before dark. We groped down a bottomless slope of soft wet snow to a steep little buttress leading to a col on the west ridge.

The brown and gold sunset saw us still high on the ridge, traversing cautiously along an apron of snow which spilled over the huge rock band above the hanging glacier. Unwilling to contemplate the descent of such an obstacle in the dark, we were forced down to a steep glacier on the far side of the mountain. A bivouac was contemplated, the cold however forced us to keep moving down and eventually the moon came out to show us a narrow high angled snow gully leading back up on to the west ridge five hundred feet above. After this heartbreaking effort the ridge thankfully broadened out. We unroped and followed it to the top of a wide couloir running down in the direction of our camp.

By this time we were moving automatically. I fell asleep at one point waiting for Alan and woke with a start having dreamed that he had passed me in the dark. I ran down several hundred feet shouting at rocks till I realised he was still above me and that I could only have closed my eyes for seconds. Realising that we had no hope of finding the tent in the dark, we bivouacked on some rocks by the side of the couloir. I was wakened by the cold just before dawn and was surprised to see the tent on its ledge a little below us. We stumbled down to it, cooked some atta, brewed some tea and flaked out for most of the next thirty-six hours.

Picking our way down to the lake and past the smoky sheilings on the alp, we cast many a backward glance at Wee Malkie. Its fluted summit, half hidden by tails of cloud, wore for us a more benign aspect than it had a few days before. The experience it had given us had intensified our appreciation of the lonely valleys it dominated. We knew nothing of and cared less about its true name, height and mountaineering history (if any). To us its charm lay in its obscurity, together with the knowledge that the world held more interesting and exotic valleys, and more remote and lovely peaks than we could visit in a lifetime.

ARRAN THIS SUMMER

By W. Skidmore

My immediate gut response on receiving orders from a persistent sub-editor to write an article on Arran was 'Why Me?' For some time now I have been quietly working away at shaking off the Arran Specialist image (usually used in a derogatory manner) by pointing out at every opportunity that I do climb in other places as well, even as far North as Glencoe and Nevis. Why, I even took on the Alps once—my performance was something to do with altitude, they said. But sub-editors are hardened to all this and what's in a label? So I more or less resigned myself to the chore of writing.

Then, in a final desperate attempt to get off the hook I recalled something about a moratorium—I looked the word up—on route descriptions somewhere. With growing indignation I worked myself up into a Don't Sell Arran frame of mind. The slogans came trotting out—'More means Worse,' 'Hell is Other People,' 'Save our Wilderness,' 'People are Pollution,' etc. I even scraped the 'Arran This Summer' sticker from the car window and only the fear of legal action from the Arran Tourist Board prevented me substituting 'Arran is a Dump.'

'The moratorium only applies to the North West,' I was told. Crushed again.

'The North West doesn't need it,' I said. 'The rain does that. Arran needs protecting from people and Glaswegians. Leave the Island Alone.'

'The Whole Club decided it was to be only the North West,' repeated the sub-editor menacingly. Mental images of A.G.M. types making speeches about agencies with scabby sounding initials and heavy responsibilities finally cracked my resistance and (natural) laziness, so I weakly agreed to Sell Out Arran.

Why does Arran inspire so many articles and books? Skye, which is supposed to be the Mecca hardly ever appears in our *Journal* except in the New Climbs section. A look at the bibliography on Arran shows an astonishing breadth of subject matter covered over the years. Certainly part of the reason is that Arran is relatively near to the main population centres but the boat service offsets this to some extent. I am convinced that some odd combination of factors is the explanation of the fascination this island holds for many people. Contrast with the up-river scene is obvious. Compactness of mountain, moor, glen, coast and population, is more striking than, say, Skye. It is a summer place second to none. The climbing is anything but straightforward yet can be addictive. Arran is all wrong in the same way as a camel is a horse designed by a committee. Whoever thought up this place did so in a distinctly mischievous frame of mind.

'Right,' I thought, 'write. Do it, but keep it disinterested in the objective style of the Southern hard men in their magazines. A minimum of personal involvement. None of this bumming your chat stuff. A clinical appraisal of Arran Now and let people discover some other way that you did a fair number of the ascents yourself—big head.'

I tried. No use. How can you write dispassionately about a place where the climbing has become inextricably bound up with so many other influences? Year after year I have camped, cottaged or caravanned with family and friends. Then there are the locals you know, characters every one. The nasty rumour that 'everybody is half cuckoo' is actually taken as a compliment. And the fishing, camp fire barbecues at midnight, it all happens if you want it—we won't go into the mixed bathing after midnight—and more besides. Rain and midges? Just another rumour.

I don't really like Arran climbing. Even the best climbs usually follow some kind of fault where moisture can linger for a long time, with or without vegetation. The rule is, the steeper the better, if you can find some holds. But there are additional problems. The climbing is often unpredictable, committing and strenuous. Seldom is it possible to look ahead and be at all confident that the next apparent hold is the real thing. Holds usually materialise where least, and vanish where most expected. This is true of any ascent but on first ascents it means the leader is in for a hard time.

This brings me to the question of aid. The nature of the climbing means that the occasional nut or peg will be used on first ascents for a breather or pull while the pioneer gets himself together. This is no apology on my part, it is simply a formula for survival—ask any-one, even the very best of rock climbers who has tried virgin Arran rock. Most things driven or slotted in are the result of an honest conviction at the time that the alternative is to fall off. Super critical modernists who find this unpalatable in other areas will find less scope in Arran for 'clean climbing.' Chalk won't help them but the modern forced training methods will. Personally I think the current move to spurn all aid is a good thing but the haughty attitude of the leading proponents can be juvenile and boring. It is also a bit dishonest since the whole trend depends more on chock protection than any great breakthrough in technique or courage. Why not say so? But I digress. The point I am trying to make is that Arran climbs are different and require certain mental adjust-ments to be enjoyable. With good dry conditions the climbs described will satisfactorily fill anyone's day.

Of the twenty-two or so new climbs done since the publication of the current Arran Rock Guide in early 1970, about half deserve serious comment. First, however, we are faced with the enigma of the one and only true winter ascent ever recorded there—*Nuis Chimney*[1]. It is surely odd that this isolated ascent should result in a superb winter line. The reason is simply that the chimney is one of the very few Arran gullies which is steep, hard and foul in summer, whereas the rest are just easy and foul. Cold enough

---

[1] *Mountain Magazine* No. 32 (1974), article and photographs.

conditions do come, and, being near the sea, can consolidate quickly. I hope someone, unlike me, took advantage of the long cold spell in February of this year to climb one or two of the worthwhile winter lines which must be there. Not that Arran can ever become a winter climbing centre in the usual sense, it will not; but neglected it certainly is.

The most important summer action has centred on the Meadow Face of Beinn Tarsuinn and the Bastion area of Cioch na h'Oighe. The former has yielded two outstanding climbs: *The Blinder*[2] and *Brobdingnag*[3]. Jim Crawford and myself built up quite a head of steam over *The Blinder* due to imagined competition and a real attempt by an English party over Easter of the same year, 1971. On our second attempt, from a high camp and in blazing hot weather which almost burned us off, we succeeded. Despite some vegetation in the middle, it is a fine, well protected, serious climb, recently improved with the elimination (by Geoff Cohen) of our couple of chock moves on pitch two. No, its name will not be changed! Being a corner line it requires good dry conditions to be enjoyable. This advice applies to all the Meadow Face routes, indeed, to almost any hard climb in Arran.

Before, during, and after our huffing and puffing on *The Blinder* we were compelled to consider the great edge to the right; now the line of *Brobdingnag*. Obviously it was a major challenge but, frankly, it frightened me and anyway it looked as if a lot of aid would be necessary. I rejected this and was left for the first time avoiding an unclimbed line on the grounds of honest-to-God fear! This careful decision of self-denial seemed fully justified when, in 1974, Rowe and Trees tackled the line via an indirect start away to the right at *Brachistochrone*. Using considerable aid they got very high on the edge only to be forced into a tension traverse left into *The Blinder*. Although an epic attempt the result must have been a disappointment after such great effort. For my own part I sat back feeling smug at not resorting to so much aid just to force the thing; it could never be a decent, mainly free line. I was right, and considered the thing exorcised.

But in the end I turned out to be wrong. The very next year saw a lot of activity on this part of the Meadow Face. The whole story is yet to be told but the result must be just about the fiercest climb yet in Arran. The story is that the lower part of the edge was climbed first, more or less direct, by Geoff Cohen and party who then seemed to vanish from the scene. Almost immediately Messrs. Duckworth, Frazer and Smith came along, and using only two or three pegs, climbed the entire thing without any escape left at the

---

[2]*S.M.C.J.*, 1972, xxx, 24, article, photographs and route description.
[3]*S.M.C.J.*, 1975, 1974, xxx, 269, 384, 393, route description and notes.

top. I have no first-hand knowledge of either the difficulty or quality of this route but just looking at it is enough to convince me that it cannot be anything else but very serious and exciting.

At this point my own connection with Arran was changing. As mentioned earlier the climbing has always seemed a bit scary to me and besides, other places called. My visits now took the form of an annual family camping holiday in Glen Sannox with no intervening weekends. The climbing was dictated by weather, mood, and availability of friends. Lower Glen Sannox is a bonny spot largely free from the Glen Rosa problems of agriculture, ponies, cattle, motor bikes and people. Mind you, the annual camp of the Third Wigan Girl Guides can be a headache but a great wind (the glen has a tunnel effect—haystacks have been known to descend on fishing boats in Sannox Bay!) of a couple of years back has kept them away. Perhaps they are still sewing! A more recent hazard has since appeared in the form of a certain kilted, overweight and elderly boy scout from Edinburgh who, without any apparent authority, insists on collecting camp fees at any time of day or night for the local farmer. At least you can spray things on midges!

Cioch na h'Oighe cannot be ignored from the Sannox camp site. Access is easy at one hour, unlike most Arran crags. The stigma of poor rock, correctly applied to the earlier climbs with one exception, has at last been lifted and the cliff can now boast of at least five excellent routes. The prime mover in this process was the late Andrew Maxfield who had a definite 'thing' about Arran and the Cioch in particular. His two main discoveries were *Tidemark* and *Klepht*, both in the current Guide Book. The former is an irresistible, good humoured severe, a traverse really, and the latter a fierce crack line, probably unrepeated since 1967. I tried and failed at the start of pitch three where the stance and belays felt inadequate for tackling the crucial corner crack which is six inches wide and holdless. We retreated using the insecure belay. Maxfield used a few unadmitted wedges on the first ascent but the advent of big chocks may give some protection nowadays. The removal of some vegetation would certainly make the line more attractive and perhaps encourage someone to prove my notion that this is a very good climb.

Meanwhile I and various friends were becoming familiar with the place, enjoying and linking the old *Midnight Ridge Direct* (the exception mentioned earlier) and *Tidemark*; all great for a short day. During this period we produced *Slipway*[4], a hard one pitch climb on the little buttress above Ledge Four, as a continuation to *Tidemark*. Time passed. Happy days, until it gradually dawned on us that the impossible looking lines to the right of *Klepht* on the

---

[4]*S.M.C.J.*, 1976, xxxi, 52, route description.

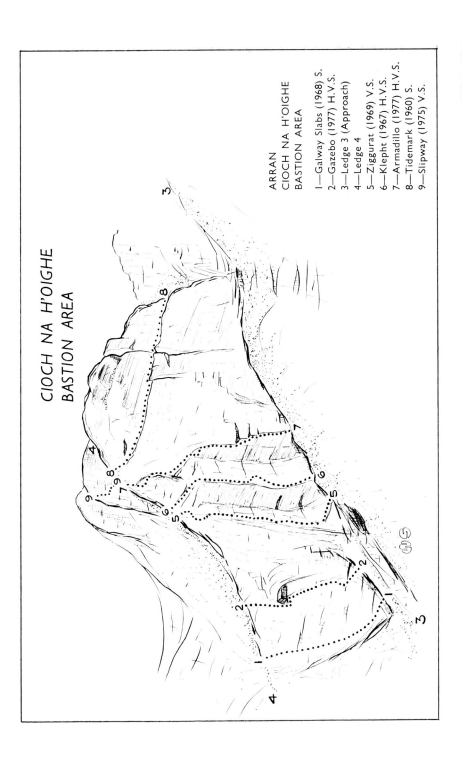

CIOCH NA H'OIGHE
BASTION AREA

ARRAN
CIOCH NA H'OIGHE
BASTION AREA

1—Galway Slabs (1968) S.
2—Gazebo (1977) H.V.S.
3—Ledge 3 (Approach)
4—Ledge 4
5—Ziggurat (1969) V.S.
6—Klepht (1967) H.V.S.
7—Armadillo (1977) H.V.S.
8—Tidemark (1960) S.
9—Slipway (1975) V.S.

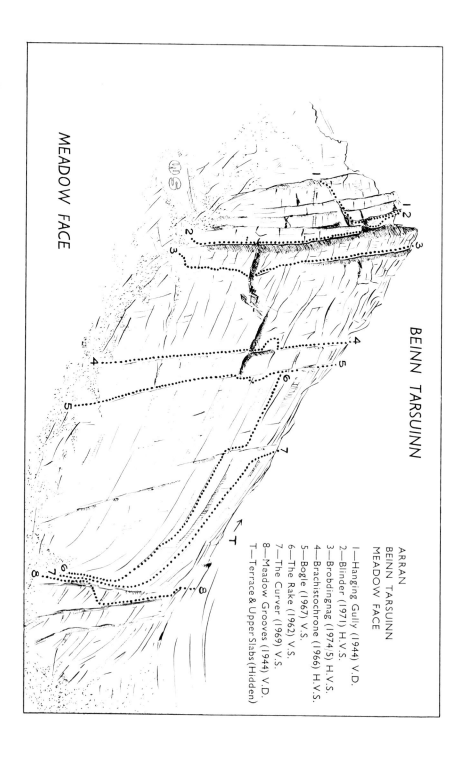

MEADOW FACE

BEINN TARSUINN

ARRAN
BEINN TARSUINN
MEADOW FACE

1—Hanging Gully (1944) V.D.
2—Blinder (1971) H.V.S.
3—Brobdingnag (1974/5) H.V.S.
4—Brachistochrone (1966) H.V.S.
5—Bogle (1967) V.S.
6—The Rake (1962) V.S.
7—The Curver (1969) V.S.
8—Meadow Grooves (1944) V.D.
T—Terrace & Upper Slabs (Hidden)

Bastion might be less improbable than we thought. Look what complacency did for us on the Meadow Face! A burning hot fortnight in July 1977 left us with no excuses.

Between bathing and boozing we first tackled the slabs left of *Ziggurat*, the lure being the inscrutable cave so obvious from the corrie and begging for exploration. The climb, *Gazebo*[5], is hard on body and brain at Hard Very Severe. Dry conditions are a must.

Satisfying as *Gazebo* was, it was really a training climb for the real thing—the ferocious roof capped corner or groove to the right of *Klepht*. I sniffed around it for days and despite a growing conviction that it was most unlikely to go I felt we had to try. Sitting in the Corrie pub one evening the 'green light' came on in my head and a quick telephone call to Bob Richardson (living off relatives in Brodick) brought him pedalling round to Sannox next morning.

It is a strange feeling standing under a climb you think may well be outwith your capabilities, especially if it has never been climbed before! I imagine it is similar to 'going over the top' in trench warfare—fear and fascination at the same time. We stood and talked in loud voices that glorious morning, stealing glances at our chosen test. The steep, clean groove and crack interrupted by roofs and bulges gave us a hard won climb of three pitches at or over Hard Very Severe. *Armadillo*[6], though not particularly long, is superb, giving Glencoe situations and good protection. The story is by no means complete as yet but I think it can be claimed that the Bastion of Cioch na h'Oighe has at last come of age.

Moving away from the Meadow Face and the Bastion the new climbs produced are a mixed bag of good, bad and downright mysterious. *Right On*[7], a 610 ft. route up the ghastly slabs and corners to the right of *Nuis Chimney* came from Ian Rowe in 1970 and required something like sixteen pegs. It is one of these routes that had to be done but will probably never be repeated. Another intriguing climb is *Voodoo Child*[8] (Little and Dykes, 1969) on the Full Meed Tower of Beinn Tarsuinn facing the Nuis cliffs. The Tower is well seen from Lower Glen Rosa and the climb takes a very attractive line despite quite a lot of aid being used. I have never heard of any second ascent.

One route I do know more about is *Stoic*[9] on Coire nan Ceum. This is a 300 ft. cyclopean wall isolated in upper North Glen Sannox and was 'discovered' by Maxfield who climbed four routes on it, all of which are in the current guide. The best of these is

[5]See New Climbs, p. 269.
[6]See New Climbs, p. 269.
[7]*S.M.C.J.*, 1971, xxix, 402, route description.
[8]*S.M.C.J.*, 1970, xxix, 284, route description.
[9]*S.M.C.J.*, 1974, xxx, 268, route description.

probably *Fuoco* with its interesting final pitch. *Entasis*, left of *Fuoco* has now been straightened out into an independent line (C. Macadam, 1975) and is no doubt improved. But all these routes are eclipsed by *Stoic* which goes more or less straight up the wall right of *Fuoco* and involves a hard mantleshelf and ramp move on the steep middle wall pitch. We found it quite gripping and look forward to a second opinion.

Of the rest, probably *Intruder* on A'Chir and *Sunshine Corner* on the Rosa Pinnacle are of real interest. Other recent climbs which I have not mentioned in areas such as the Lower Rosa Pinnacle, Rosa Slabs, A'Chir and the Lower Slabs of Caisteal Abhail, are of no great merit as far as I know. Such routes are inevitable on Arran and will continue to appear *ad nauseam* (now there's a good route name!) where so much indifferent rock exists. However they at least show that climbers are looking for new ground and maybe a few more plums will be discovered in the process. Meantime the object of this article is to help climbers avoid disappointment by describing the best of the recent climbs on a unique island.

Arran is so unique that it is a matter of permanent amazement to me that the Club has never made a really serious effort to obtain a climbing hut in Rosa or Sannox. Some members brush the idea aside by pointing out that the two Glens are ideal for camping but this argument could equally be applied to Glencoe and Skye, where we already consider huts to be desirable. Glen Rosa is no longer the good campsite it once was, as I explained earlier, unless the camp is well up the Glen. Time is limited on Arran mainly due to the boat service and high camping, however pleasant, is an additional factor in a already tight timetable. I would forecast that the days of pleasant camping on Arran are numbered. If the funds and suitable property could be found or built (and any such scheme would be expensive) I would make a strong plea that no better investment could be made than an S.M.C. hut on the Island of Arran.

GRIPPED IN THE CRYPT

By Philip Gribbon

THEY stood and counted the caves of Bidean nan Bian. Daft was doing the outmoded v.diffs made by ancient climbers on obscure crags and Auld Dawg had come to humour him in his collection of vintage routes. A brace of the archaic classics lay on Churchdoor Buttress.

Once on a fine alpine day they had climbed the splintered door jamb of Flake route to find a teetering concertina of cracked keystones and vacuous holes waiting for their careful steps in the sunshine. The shattered bridge that spanned the buttress has created the impression of a gigantic ecclesiastical archway that leads into the mountain.

Once again they stood and cogitated. Which one of the gaping holes amongst the battered blocks in the long chimney was the entrance to Crypt route? Daft tried to digest a traditional account of tunnels and passages, Auld Dawg looked at the dots on the pictures and counted numerals and triple asterisks, and the young lad peered at the black slots, waiting expectantly. Drizzle drifted across the corrie.

'Och, there's nothing for it,' grumbled Auld Dawg. 'Straight up. We'll find the right cave somewhere.'

It was time to start the explorations. Gathering a garland of tapes, Daft spread his legs and bridged up into a forgotten niche. His voice betrayed his disappointment. 'It goes nowhere, except out again.' He appeared, writhing sinuously, and having draped a blue talisman on a spike, clawed at a daunting set of cracks, wriggled sideways, and was engulfed in the rock. 'I'm on a platform in a sort o' cave, an' there's room for everyone.'

'What shape is it?' enquired Auld Dawg.

'Well, ah . . .' Daft didn't see that it made any difference.

'Is it a gallery? Measuring six by twenty by four feet?' quoted Auld Dawg, with misplaced confidence in the guide book.

'What? It's ah . . . .' mumbled Daft impatiently. 'C'mon.'

They struggled after him. There wasn't an obvious continuation within the mountain, but an uninviting pothole dropped to the unknown depths and a window led to the sky. 'I'll try the outside way,' suggested Daft as he bridged up towards the daylight.

'It's not that way,' said Auld Dawg pointedly as Daft disappeared from view. 'We've missed the entrance somehow.'

Auld Dawg took his torch and looked cautiously into the pothole. Loose scree rattled down the abyss. Astride the void he noticed a curving chimney rising inside the shaft. Ah, the secret passage to our goal, he thought, and quickly shuffled back to a safer stance.

'It's your turn,' he informed the disconsolate Daft who was resting after a fruitless search. 'I'll go.'

Daft took to the shaft as directed. The rope ran out, and his commentary was stifled. Sounds began to come from another direction. With his head on one side, Auld Dawg could hear sustained scrapings coming closer. Daft was inventing a new circular path that looped back inside the hill. 'Go back the way you came, ya silly . . . .' but his brain failed to find a suitable description for his companion.

Once more they assembled in their cave. Auld Dawg reconsidered the external route, was appalled by a forbidding cleft rising bleakly up the wall and from which a chill spray of water cast its sheet of derision on his hopes, and pretending to look for a cave he ran up a side wall into a cul-de-sac.

'It's ridiculous! Three attempts, an' we're still here,' he declared vehemently on his return, and sat looking morosely out at the grey clouds. 'We've lost it, afore we've even found it,' he complained, expressing his feeling of dejection. 'One last keek at the back, an' then we'll jack it in.'

He worked into a dim corner, and tentatively stuck his wandering fingers up a crevice. Open sesame! He felt nothing except emptiness. His torch revealed the lost crypt. He was to endure silent ecstasy, as discomforted by brutal spikes, he immersed himself within the uncertain clamp of a sightless tomb in a world blotted out by tangible darkness. His eyes became accustomed to his plight. Slowly he sensed a faint glimmering that flickered a vision of light in the sky, the reality at the end of an infinite distance. 'Eureka!' he cried, and plunged unwittingly into a fissure. 'Troglodytes rule!'

Frantically he wriggled along the narrow chimney, fearful that huge splinters might crash off the roof, and footholds might tumble through the floor. He memorised scanty holds on the wet walls and stuffed his torch into his shirt. He thrashed at his converging prison walls, fighting them back with his elbows and knees, shoving with his shoulder and blocking with his bottom. At last the exit hole was nearly within reach. With strenuous struggles he won a few frustrating feet. He squeezed to the side and tried not to breathe. By burrowing horizontally he imitated a maverick mole, but failed dismally to gain an inch. It was obvious that some of his statistics were incompatible with further progress. He pushed backwards, exposing a bare midriff. His route now was downwards, sliding back to the belay. 'It's no go. It's too small,' he declared miserably. 'Let's go home.'

'The book claims it's eighteen inches wide, an' surely we can get through that.'

'Humph!' said Auld Dawg, refraining from coarse language. 'That's rubbish. Either it's a misprint, or the mountain is shrinking.'

Although the young lad, befitting a novice in the presence of his betters, had been quiet all day, now he diffidently suggested, 'Can I have a look?'

'Sure, feel free,' snapped Auld Dawg with marked disinterest. 'Go ahead, try it.'

The slight figure vanished into the hole and the rope rushed out. A scent of success came from within the rock. 'There's a light above me, an' a chimney going straight up.'

What on earth had he found in there? Some dark diversion, thought Auld Dawg in baffled surprise, that he had missed with eyes open but with his mind blank. The late afternoon had caught a vital spark.

'I'll go on,' said the voice.

'Good man, do that,' exhorted Auld Dawg passionately, 'an' hurry up,'

They watched as the rope wormed away steadily with its coils, clambering across the platform.

'There's a hole . . . . out in . . . . the wall.'

'Can you get out?'

'I think so,' came the doubtful reply.

They waited, patient and hopeful, aware of the drama enacted within the rock.

'It should be no bother.' Daft believed in printed words. 'It says the maximum diameter is eighteen inches.'

'I'm through!' A weak throttled cry of elation seeping from the entrance.

'Great!' muttered Auld Dawg in a flurry of activity. 'With only one rope, I'll tie on now, you take the end, an' both move together, otherwise we're here for the night.'

He was through the hole before Daft realised what was happening, but there he was stopped, thwarted by his pack. The solution was to tie it on ahead and push it up the chimney. He grovelled onwards with Daft grunting at his heels. He saw his own impenetrable exit hole, and then he had a premonition, a strange *deja vu* feeling of frustration allied to imminent disillusionment. A tiny head was framed in the exit. 'Oh no, he's gone up the bloody selfsame hole, the crazy kite . . . . Would you believe it? Curses! Away from this soddin' route . . . . at once. It's impossible!' Wings of insanity were fluttering in stygian bloom.

They went into retreat, spinning and straddling down the chimney cracks, to slither and slide down the gully, regaining a highland corrie where the dusky rain lashed the black buttresses of Bidean and drove them thankfully down the track towards the Clachaig . . . .

'You're buying.' Daft and the young lad had caught up with Auld Dawg beside the burn. 'We're looking forward to a couple o' pints,' he gasped, '. . . . at least . . . . each. Otherwise . . . .'

'Okay, sounds fine,' was the cautious reply, 'But what about . . . . otherwise?'

'We'll say you couldn't get up 'cos you're too fat.'

'What nonsense!' sneered Auld Dawg, and trotted off disdainfully, with a prospecting pat at his waistline.

'It's my chest that's too big. I've never had such an insult, an' blackmail won't get you anywhere, 'cos the book's wrong. It's my chest, I say . . . .'

ENERGY DEVELOPMENTS AND THE SCOTTISH LANDSCAPE

By D. J. Bennet

As was shown at the most recent Annual General Meeting of the Club, our members (like the majority of climbers in Scotland) have a lively interest in the possible impact of technological developments in Scotland on our landscape, in particular the landscape of the mountains and wilderness areas. This concern has also been voiced in meetings of the Mountaineering Council of Scotland and the Scottish Countryside Activities Council which I have recently attended.

Our natural inclination as climbers is to resist any development which we perceive to have a detrimental affect on the landscape, but I suspect that in resisting one development we may often pay little or no attention to the wider consequences should our opposition be successful and some alternative development be necessary as a result.

Nowhere is this dilemma more real than in the field of energy production and use, and in particular the generation of electrcity. I assume that most of us would agree that overall energy production must continue in this country at least at the present level, and more likely at a modest rate of growth. If we do not accept this, we must consider our own position. Are we prepared to use less energy and energy related products? As climbers, we tend to take for granted unlimited supplies of petrol to get us to the mountains at weekends, and I suspect we run up a bigger than average annual mileage in doing so. In other words we may well be using more than our fair share of that soon-to-become scarce energy product—petrol, and we are not in a sound moral position to urge restraint in other areas of energy use.

Drastic changes in life-style designed to bring about reduced energy use are not a feasible proposition, though we may well be forced to change our own climbing life-style in the not-too-distant future, and return by cycle to the hills of our childhood—the Campsies and Pentlands.

In the field of electricity generation the generating boards have a responsibility to meet the fluctuating requirements of domestic and industrial users at the minimum price, and still have adequate reserves to meet emergencies. There are several sources of energy for electricity generation—oil, coal, uranium and the sun through the agency of winds, waves and rain. Forget oil, it is too valuable to burn in power stations. Coal is plentiful but dirty, and the hazards of the emissions from coal fired power stations are quite significant, though we have always tended to gloss over them. (More sulphur dioxide from our power stations finishes up in Scandinavia than ever falls down on our own towns and fields).

That brings us to uranium—nasty dangerous stuff, or is it? Ask any Aberdonian, for the radiation levels from uranium in the buildings of the Granite City are higher than at the perimeter of a nuclear power station. Uranium at present provides adequate supplies of the cheapest and cleanest electricity available to us, provided the problem of the ultimate disposal of the radioactive waste can be solved, so we should not reject it too readily, particularly as no better alternative is presently available.

The problem of the ultimate disposal of this waste is so important that it merits careful and detailed research. One possibility is disposal deep underground in stable geological regions, and the test drillings proposed in Galloway and elsewhere are part of a ten-year programme of research being carried out in several areas of Western Europe to find suitable sites for disposal. I would rather see this research done now to prepare for the solution of this problem than find ourselves in ten years time with the disposal problem on our hands and no adequate preparations made to deal with it. If the time eventually comes when a site is chosen in this country, I think we will find that on the surface at least it is not unduly obtrusive. As an indication of the scale of the disposal operation, I estimate that if all the U.K's electricity requirements were produced from nuclear sources, the annual volume of glassified waste to be disposed of would be about 130 cubic metres. This is a fairly small operation and unlikely to have much environmental impact above ground, trivial by comparison with the mining of an equivalent amount of coal and disposing of the mine waste and ash.

The increased use of solar energy is the present aim of engineers, and it is a goal which we should all endorse, but let us not overlook some of the implications. Hydro-electricity is the most obvious example of solar energy at work in Scotland, and the visual impact of reservoirs, dams and power stations is considerable. We seem to have learned to live with these, and have played a part in successfully opposing schemes which would have been disasters from a scenic point of view, such as Glen Nevis.

Electricity from wind power is another proposed scheme, and we in Scotland are certainly well-endowed with exposed and windy sites for aero-generators. (We have about 90% of the U.K. potential). If this source of energy were exploited we might, at a rather optimistic estimate, generate half of Scotland's electricity from it at a cost considerably higher than present costs, and with the disadvantage that, because winds are intermittent, we would still have to have conventional power stations to provide electricity on windless days. Now think of the environmental impact: the estimate given above is based on the installation of about ten thousand aero-generators on coastal, moorland and hill-top sites, each aero-generator as large as the biggest transmission pylon, but unlike the pylons which to a large extent are situated in valleys, the aero-generators would be on the most visually obtrusive sites. What would you think if every Munro was crowned by a pylon 30 metres high with its 46-metre diameter rotor whirling in the wind? And don't forget the thousands of pylons and miles of transmission lines that would link these generators to the grid. The mind boggles.

Next, we can think of wave power. There is no doubt that the energy of the waves which pound the beaches of the Hebrides could, if harnessed and transmitted to the mainland, satisfy Scotland's electricity needs, with some to spare to sell to England. But the technical problems are a long way from solution, and the environmental impact would be great. One visualises this impact as being a number of power collecting stations in the Hebrides with possibly industries set up there to produce electricity-intensive products such as hydrogen, transmission lines to a point where a submarine cable would lead to Skye, and more transmission lines through Skye and down the length of the western Highlands to the centres of population. By comparison, the power line to Skye which we discussed a couple of years ago seems insignificant. Wave energy suffers from the same disadvantage as wind energy—its intermittent and rather unpredictable nature—and it would be necessary to have other power stations available for calm days, or alternatively electricity storage schemes.

Finally, the mention of storage schemes brings us to this subject. Whether a country's electricity generation system is based on large nuclear power stations operating at constant output (and this is the most economical way to use uranium), or on wind and wave energy generators which have unpredictably fluctuating outputs, there is a need for energy storage systems which will enable supply to meet demand at all times. The alternative is to use small intermittently-operating power stations which (hydro-electric schemes excepted) produce expensive electricity. The only practical method of storing large quantities of energy at present is by pumped storage hydro-electric schemes, and there are two such schemes already operating in Scotland, at Foyers and Cruachan. The N.S.H.E.B. has plans for more, and in particular proposes to build a large scheme at Craigroyston on the east side of Loch Lomond, creating in the process a new reservoir at the head of the Cailness Burn just below the summit of Ben Lomond on its north side. Predictably, these proposals have given rise to protests from many quarters and for many different reasons. One obvious suggestion has been that the existing Loch Sloy scheme should be modified and enlarged to become a pumped storage scheme, but this proposal has been rejected apparently on the grounds of greater cost. No-one seems to have seriously asked how much extra the public might be prepared to pay for its electricity in order to preserve the environment of places like Ben Lomond, but if the question were asked and answered it would show where society's priorities lie.

To return to Craigroyston, however, I do not think that the scheme itself will be unduly offensive in the visual sense—certainly a great deal less so than the Cruachan scheme. There will be a small reservoir, a few miles of new road, partly screened by the growing forest on Craigroyston, a low dam which will be practically invisible from below and about three miles of pylons to reach the existing power line from Glasgow to Cruachan, with which the new line will go in parallel. There will be other effects (particularly during the construction period) in villages such as Drymen and Balmaha, and the long term effect of a widened road from Drymen to Rowardennan will almost certainly be to attract more folk to the east side of Loch Lomond. Is this a good or bad thing? We are told that Loch Lomond is the great 'fresh air lung' for the people of Glasgow, the place on their doorstep where they can get into unspoilt, wild country. If this is the case, why not provide them with a decent road?

One contribution that climbers, through their clubs, the M.C. of S. and S.C.A.C. should make is to insist that when construction of some major scheme is finished and contractors depart, the site is properly tidied up and if necessary landscaped. We should never again tolerate the mess that was left behind in Coiregrogain after the Sloy scheme was built.

In conclusion, although we should certainly keep our eyes on the activities of the power boys, we should not as a matter of routine criticise all their plans. Let us be selective in our opposition and reserve it for the really deserving cases such as, for example, a pumped storage scheme in the Letterewe mountains. Finally, a word of warning. You may think the power boys are bad; the ones I fear are the Dutch property speculators, making their quick and easy profits from vast tracts of north-west highland landscape such as (dare one suggest it) Letterewe.

GERIATRIC RHYMES

We're the geriatric mountaineers, the septuagenarians;
All younger climbers we regard as immature barbarians.
In days of yore when we were young climbing was most respectable
And all the peaks were virginal—immaculate—delectable;
No pitons scarred the rock face, no beer cans soiled the corries,
No ski lifts reared their ugly heads when we went on our forays
With Sherlock Holmesish head gear and belted Norfolk jackets,
And six foot alpenstocks in hand and boots so full of tackets
That sparks flew out from every rock, igneous or sedimentary.
We talked in their own language to all the landed gent(a)ry;
Their keepers standing cap in hand were everywhere obsequious,
The very deer expressed delight to be on the same peak wi' us!

We had our little quiet jokes but frowned upon vulgarity—
The silence of the lonely hills discouraged cheap hilarity,
And we had come to understand what Wordsworth and what Byron
In all those lovely poems on the mountainous environment. [meant
Our hearts leapt up at rainbows, and to men of education
There's not the meanest flower that blows but brings its apt quotation.

And so we tramped the mountainside and on into the distance,
And sometimes reached a summit—by the line of *least* resistance.
But when rocks above got steepish or the thick mists proved
                                                    [bewild'ring
A vision flashed before us of our sorrowing wives and childring—
A vision that inspired us to fresh effort and activity,
And very quickly took us to the foot of the declivity
And home to where our prattling babes received us with felicity,
And the anxious 'Little Woman' wrapped us round in domesticity.

And thus we have survived to be the septuagenarians
Compared with whom all younger mountaineers are but barbarians
Who fail to show respect to older men of proved ability,
Intelligence and enterprise, discretion—*and* gentility.
But were it not for modesty that borders on humility
We'd tell you tales remembered—and embellished!—in tranquility
Of desperate adventures in the days of our virility,
When Mummery paid tribute to our climbing versatility
And even Whymper envied us our courage and agility;
And—but enough! The world today lacks reverence and civility
And treats our tales—and verses—as the maunderings of senility.

B.F.S.

NEW CLIMBS SECTION

GUIDES and GRADINGS.—Events move faster than anticipated. A new series of Rock Guides, covering the whole of Scotland and selective, (if not discriminating in nature), will begin to be seen in late 1979, with the publication of the Glencoe Guide (see p. 291). These guides will be innovative in many ways, and must stand for a few years at least. Because of this, but more so due to the recent rise in rock standards seen recently in Scotland (see Notes for *Freak-Out* and *Titan's Wall*, etc.), we boldly go where no Scot has gone before, and extend the grading system to include Extremely Severe. We hope to publish a list of routes regraded into this category in the next issue.

METRICATION rears its head. Arising as spin-off (drop-off?) from the French Revolution, it may be time to bend with most of the rest of the world and shorten all these long routes we have. Those who can afford it buy their ropes in 45 m. lengths anyway. Serious comments are invited from active climbers, foot-weary or otherwise. The next issue will include metric equivalents.

CREDITS for route makers. In the last issue we proposed an ingenious system of notation involving a + sign where appropriate. There has been opposition; and we publish a letter which argues against such arid exactitude. We invite comment and if support for the modification is not forthcoming we shall revert to the former practice.

NEW CLIMBS—ARRAN

Glen Sannox: Cioch na h'Oighe.—*Armadillo*.   350 ft.   Hard Very Severe.

W. Skidmore + R. Richardson. 14th July 1977.

This route climbs the impressive, roofed corner crack right of *Klepht*. Climb corner direct to middle roof, turn this on left (2 pegs) to gain ledge and belays under third roof (80 ft.). Continue in groove over remarkable rock splinter (shaky, but not vital), to top, traverse left (lower line) from runner to grass ledge. Climb awkward slab wall to grass rake which follow up over left rock scar to belay (130 ft.). Climb series of short, overhung corners with hard move on right wall near start to gain grass ledge. Traverse left, up, then right into final easy grass groove and flake belay a few feet down ledge 4 from the finish of *Tidemark* (140 ft.). Recommended.

—*Gazebo*.   350 ft.   Hard Very Severe.

W. Skidmore + A. Walker. 5th July 1977.

This route lies midway between *Galway Slabs* and *Ziggurat*. The prominent feature is a large roof and cave at the end of pitch two. Start on ledge three just down from diagonal overlap.

Climb short groove and slab above to overlap. Continue up slab (delicate) or take to raised narrow slab above overlap (strenuous), until possible to move up right to grass ledge and belay (peg runner used, 90 ft.). Follow obvious corner to good stance and belay in cave, hard section near top (130 ft.). Drop down left to lower slab, move up to overlap then traverse left round corner into groove leading by heather and crumbly rock to ledge four and belay at rock scar (130 ft.).

A'Chir: Coire Daingean—*Na Ciste*.   460 ft. Very Severe.
W. McKerrow, D. Nichols, A. Nisbet & G. S. Strange. 5th June 1977.

Climbs No. 6 – 7 buttress fairly centrally. Start at lowest slabs, below and right of obvious vertical turf-filled crack. Climb slab to top of short heather corner on right. Move right and go up to belay on flakes. Move back left on to slab and climb it to terrace. Continue up leftwards behind large flake on to slab. Traverse this right and up to next terrace. Move right and climb up rightwards on flake holds until possible to gain next terrace. Climb wall via flake crack on left. Directly above is a fault formed by detached blocks. Climb this to small platform. Traverse right then go up leftwards by short layback crack. Move left and pull over final bulge on good holds.

SKYE I

Coire Lagan: Sròn na Ciche: Eastern Buttress.—*Dilemma*.
M. Fowler & P. Thomas. 21st June 1977.   260 ft. Extremely Severe.

This route climbs the slab and overhang between *Vulcan Wall* and *Creag Dubh Grooves*. Start at the thin crack in the slab between these routes. Climb crack until possible to traverse horizontally left to the stance above pitch one of *Vulcan Wall* (60 ft.). Regain and climb crack to its finish then climb up right to overlap, climb under overlap into faint groove then climb overlap to gain a descending traverse line leading to a small niche just left of the large stance on *Creag Dubh Grooves* (90 ft.). Follow the crack diagonally left up the slab, then its continuation through the overhangs to the top (110 ft.).

Sgùrr MhicCoinnich: West Face.—*The Twister*.
C. & S. Rowland. February 1978.   1,000 ft. GRADE III.

This follows the wide, shallow gully immediately to the left of, and parallel to, the *West Buttress* route. The vertical step at mid height was turned on the left.

SKYE II

Coireachan Ruadha: Sgùrr MhicCoinnich.—*Populace*.
N. Muir & A. Paul. 12th August 1977.   600 ft. Very Severe.

On the left wall of *North East Gully* is a very obvious corner system. The climb follows the corners for 350 ft. to where the system splits in two; the right hand being a very steep V-groove, the left a steep chimney. Climb chimney to exit onto slab (150 ft.). Above an obvious fault splits the final buttress. Climb this to finish on summit ridge (100 ft.).

Blaven: East Face.—*Stairway to Heaven*.   400 ft. Extremely Severe.
M. Fowler & P. Thomas. 19th June 1977.

Climbs the huge wall between *Jib* and *The Great Prow*. Start at the foot of a deep groove which narrows to a crack, some 50 ft. left of the normal start to *Jib*. (Part of the first pitch had been climbed previously using aid, as a variation start to *Jib*).

Climb the groove, then a wide crack through the *Jib* traverse to a stance in a niche (100 ft.). Follow the crack to another niche (60 ft.). Move up to a fault line, follow this leftwards until possible to climb overhang via short crack, traverse right to narrow ledge above overhangs then diagonally up right to short crack leading to stance and peg belays (100 ft.). Follow crack, climb overlap and move up to a ledge. Finish up to the right (140 ft.).

NORTHERN HIGHLANDS I

Beinn Lair: North Face: Butterfly Buttress.—*Cabbage White.*
R. McHardy & A. Nisbet. 18th February 1978.   1,000 ft. GRADE III/IV.

   The first gully left of the amphitheatre running the full height of the cliff. A short, steep ice step is prominent and marks the start of the difficulties. Above this the route moves right and back left into the main line. Near the top the right hand of two branches was taken. The gully held snow but little ice, giving awkward rock moves.

—North Summit Buttress.
J. Anderson, R. McHardy, A. Nisbet & J. Unwin.   1,400 ft. GRADE III.

19th February 1978.

   An excellent route, as per guidebook prediction. A detailed description is avoided since much of the enjoyment was in route finding. After a start up an ice runnel, the route trended generally left.

Easter Ross: The Fannichs: Sgùrr nan Clach Geala.—

Skyscraper Buttress. 800 ft. GRADE V.
R. J. Archbold, M. J. Freeman, J. C. Higham & R. A. Smith. 18th February

1978. 8 hours.

   Summer route followed throughout. Following the initial section in *Gamma Gully*, the buttress gave excellent climbing on partially consolidated snow.

Number 2 Buttress.—*Sunrise Buttress.*
P. R. Baines & D. M. Nichols. 18th February 1978.   500 ft. GRADE IV.

   This route follows a line in the centre of the buttress. Start at foot of *Beta Gully*, climb ice bulges for three pitches, then obvious gully system. Turn overhang at top on left then up arête to top.

Alladale: The Alladale Wall: The Central Buttress.—*Guano Slabs.*
N. Muir & A. Paul. 15th June 1977.   800 ft. Very Difficult.

   This route takes a direct line between *Whigmaleerie* and *Rumble*. Go straight up to a point above the left hand end of the 'slanting overhanging crack' mentioned in *Whigmaleerie*. From this point can be seen a prominent nose on the skyline; climb to this in two pitches, continue more easily to top.

Corriemulzie: Seana Braigh: Luchd Coire.—*Flowerpot Buttress.*
P. Devlin & D. Dinwoodie. 16th February 1978.   900 ft. GRADE III.

   This climbs the broad buttress between *Press-On* and *Pomegranate Gullies*. It took a good natural line near the well defined right edge. The route crosses a big raking terrace at three-quarter's height, then a direct continuation to the top.

—Pineapple Gully.
P. F. Macdonald, C. & S. Rowland. 21st January 1978.   650 ft. GRADE III.

   The gully on the left flank of *Diamond Buttress*. Enter it by climbing the right wall of *Pomegranate Gully*, starting a short distance below the first pitch of that gully.

Feich Coire.—*Eagle Gully.*
D. Dinwoodie & A. McIvor; P. Devlin & G. Thompson. 800 ft. GRADE II/III.

15th February 1978.

   This turned out to be an anticlimax (see Guide, p. 159). Old snow and ice was smothered with deep, fresh snow. There remained a fair ice pitch near the start and a short, easy pitch below the top.

NORTHERN HIGHLANDS II

Beinn Eighe: Coire Mhic Fhearchair: Eastern Ramparts.—*Forge.*
N. Muir & A. Paul. 19th August 1977.   400 ft. Very Severe.

About 100 ft. left of *Rampart* is a large, pale corner with a rock scar on top. Start at foot of corner. Climb corner, traverse left at mid-height, continue up wall to belay at *Girdle Traverse*. Climb up and right of huge roof, then step left to gain chimney crack. Follow crack to ledge and block belay. Climb steep wall above and continue by grooves to top.

—*Rampage.*
N. Muir & A. Paul. 18th August 1977.   400 ft. Very Severe.

This climb lies between *Boggle* and *Samurai*, and features a pale coloured wall in its upper half, just right of a prominent, square cut roof at mid-height. Some 20 ft. right of *Boggle* is a prominent steep crack. Climb crack for 60 ft. then move right to climb groove formed by large pinnacle. Belay on top of pinnacle at *Girdle Traverse*. Climb up and right to belay on top of second pinnacle. Climb up for 20 ft. to small recess. Move up and right to gain groove, climb this to block formed ledge, belay. At left end of ledge is a chimney, well seen from below. Climb chimney to top.

East Buttress: Sandstone Tier.
—*Mango.* 250 ft. Very Severe.
N. Muir & A. Paul. 17th August 1977.

Start 40 ft. left of *The Chimney* at a small overhang. Climb up to groove, passing loose block. Move to the right groove, swing left and up to belay ledge at 150 ft. Continue up rightwards to easier ground.

West Buttress: East Face:
Quartzite Tier.—*Twilight Zone.* 600 ft. Very Severe.
N. Muir & A. Paul. 18th August 1977.

This route climbs the centre of the steep east face, passing the large roofs near the top on the left. Start in *West Central Gully* at centre of small buttress, where quartzite begins (arrow). Climb cracks and grooves to belay at first terrace (150 ft.). Climb open corner to belay at large pinnacle (50 ft.). Climb pinnacle and groove behind until forced into second groove, follow this to *Girdle* ledge and belay. Go round right 10 ft. and continue up grooves and steep slabs to spike belay (60 ft). Move left and gain groove leading to large roof, climb groove to 30 ft. below roof, step left and climb steep wall to belay at left end of roof. Climb left arête to corner and finish.

Central Wall.—*Pelican.*
N. Muir & A. Paul. 17th August 1977.   350 ft. Severe.

To the right of Patey's *Direct Route* is a prominent, steep chimney crack line. Climb this to top.

Coire Rudha-Staca: Creag Mhór.
The Pineapple Chimney. 350 ft. Very Severe.
Miss B. Clough, A. Nisbet & M. Thorp. 15th October 1977.

This route climbs the chimney formed by the right hand side of the monolith known as *The Independent Pineapple*. Only the final pitch is V.S. Follow the *Chockstone Gully* until a narrow traverse ledge leads left to the foot of the chimney. The chimney gives magnificent climbing to the top of the pinnacle, then climb the wall above for 20 ft. when an awkward move right leads round a corner (crux). Finish more easily.

—Autumn Rib.

S. Ackerly & A. Nisbet. 17th October 1977. 300 ft. Severe.

At the eastern end of the cliff are three chimneys: the right hand one having a deep cave at its foot. The two left hand chimneys are separated by a rib which becomes well defined at a platform some 50 ft. up. This route climbs the rib. Start up a deep, narrow chimney well to the left (slightly loose). The rib itself, though short, is sustained and on good rock.

Liathach: North East Coire of Spidean.—*Poacher's Fall.*

R. McHardy & A. Nisbet. 11th February 1978. 600 ft. GRADE V.

This is the large icefall which forms at the back of the coire. It gave sustained, technical climbing. Rock belays but ice screws only for runners.

Fuar Tholl: South East Cliff.—*Fuar Folly.* 750 ft. GRADE V.

R. J. Archbold & D. M. Nichols. 19th February 1978.

This approximates to the line of *Boat Tundra*, and makes a rising line from right to left on the lower left hand half of the cliff. It is sustained and steep with some good situations. Start below obvious corner of *Boat Tundra*. Trend up to right by groove/ramp to start of snow shelf. Go straight up and step right to foot of great rock bastion. Traverse left round nose to recess at foot of corner. Climb corner on ice, peg for aid (20 ft.), then leave corner for great face on left. The face is climbed in two pitches and gave the hardest climbing, aiming for a notch in the skyline. After the notch continue trending left for three pitches. Climbed on hard snow.

Ben More Coigach: Sgùrr an Fhidhleir.—*G String.*

R. McHardy & P. Thomas. Summer 1977. 800 ft. Hard Very Severe.

This climb lies about 250 ft. right of *The Magic Bow*, and starts from a good rock ledge level with the foot of the groove of that route. Gain this ledge by a series of walls and ledges which become more continuous about 200 ft. below the ledge. Above the ledge is steep rock, bounded on the right by a series of right trending overhangs. Climb to a bulge at about 45 ft., climb bulge moving right to gain a slab. Go right, then up 15 ft., go left to good ledge and belay. Above is a groove going up to the left of a block overhang. Above and left of this is another block overhang; the two separated by a groove. Enter the groove using a flake on the lower overhang and move right onto steep slabs. Move up and right to a small but long ledge, enter groove above from the right and so to good stance and peg belay. Climb straight up to big ledge, move right and round into grass filled corner. Climb thin slab on right to belay. Climb up and right over a bulge, enter a corner, finish by a wide crack on left wall.

Beinn Bhàn: Coir' Each.—*Deep Gully.* 650 ft. GRADE IV.

D. M. Jenkins & P. F. Macdonald. February 1978.

The deep snow gully in the centre of the coire. There is a large ice pitch at two-thirds height.

Coire na Poite.—*Moonshine.* 1,400 ft. GRADE IV.

D. M. Jenkins & C. Stead. 19th February 1978.

Start below the central ice falls on the back wall. Climb direct to rock barrier at 600 ft. Traverse left 150 ft. into rightward trending groove which follow, to rejoin previous line.

—Alice's Buttress.   1,100 ft.   GRADE III/IV.

R. J. Archbold & J. C. Higham.   11th February 1978.

The buttress immediately left of *March Hare Gully.* Start on left side of buttress toe. Climb diagonally right up snow ramp to a point overlooking the gully (120 ft.). Trend diagonally left then climb more or less directly to a rock band at about 750 ft. Beneath this, traverse left round a nose then go up steeply to gain the crest on the right. Follow the crest to meet the upper connecting ridge about 150 ft. below the plateau.

Sgùrr a'Chaorachain: A'Choich: Upper Tier.—*Mantissa.*

R. J. Archbold & D. Dinwoodie.   October 1975.   450 ft.   Very Severe.

First pitch as for *The Maxilla* (60 ft.). Climb crack just right of stance, cross rib rightwards into large recess (40 ft.). Leave on right and traverse right for about 40 ft. below a very steep, concave wall (this is a continuation of the smooth band mentioned in *North Climb*). Start up faint rib with cracks and continue, making move right near the top of the wall. Move left to belay (100 ft.). Trend diagonally left through overlaps to gain skyline edge (80 ft.). Continue directly to easier ground.

NORTHERN HIGHLANDS III

An Teallach: Toll an Lochain.—*The* 1978 *Face Route.*

M. Freeman & N. Keir.   19th February 1978.   1,500 ft.   GRADE III/IV.

On the main face of Corrag Bhuide there is a snow patch—*The Triangle.* This is set above a rock barrier. From the terrace below the rock barrier, reached directly from the lochan, access is possible at either base angle of *The Triangle*, or more directly by icefalls depending from the snowfield. The route then follows a rightward sloping ramp above *The Triangle* to reach the crest of the buttress which finishes to the immediate left of *Lord Berkeley's Seat.* Technical difficulties are concentrated in the final section up the crest to the main ridge. Care should be taken on a sunny day from falling ice.

Bidean A'Ghlas Thuill.—*The Alley.*

R. Baker & A. McCord.   18th December 1976.   1,200 ft.   GRADE II/III.

The gully between *Main* and *Minor Ribs.* The gully was well defined in the lower 800 ft. and contained four short ice pitches. A rock step and ramp led to the ridge.

Quinag: The Western Cliffs.—*Toby.*   500 ft.   Very Severe.

D. Gardner & A. Paul.   9th July 1977.

Left of the waste pipe are three buttresses. The following route lies on the clean cut right edge of the third. Start at the lowest rocks and climb to grassy ledge and belay. Climb edge turning nose at 50 ft. on right, continue up edge to small stance. Step left and climb cracked wall to roof. Move left, climb bulge and continue to belay. Scramble to top.

September, 1977

Photo: Hamish M. Brown

Nanda Devi from the Changabang Glacier

September, 1977

Point 6401 from the Changabang Glacier—*The route described is to the col on the left and then by the ridge to the summit*

Photo: Donald Mill

Foinaven: Creagh Dubh: Coire Duaill.—*Seers Corner.*

D. Gardner & A. Paul. 11th August 1977. 600 ft. Very Severe.

Climbs the central slabs mentioned in District Guide. In the middle of the slabs is a sizeable corner bounded on the left by a red wall. Start at light-coloured slab directly below corner. Climb slab to foot of white tongue of rock, continue up this and cross overlap to enter groove leading to spike belay in recess. Continue up corner in two pitches, when easier climbing leads to top.

—*Sava.* 400 ft. Severe.

D. Gardner & A. Paul. 11th August 1977.

On the left hand section of the crag is a sweep of overlapping slabs. The route follows the obvious crack and groove system bounding the slabs on the left. Evidence of previous parties was found. Scramble to start then follow cracks and grooves to large grass ledge. Step left and climb corner and cracks above to large prominent corner, climb this to belay near top. Continue by groove above and go directly up by flake cracks to top.

CAIRNGORMS I

The Northern Corries: Coire an Lochan: Number 2 Buttress.

—*Andromeda.* GRADE III/IV.

B. Barton & J. C. Higham. 30th December 1971. 4 hours.

This route climbs the front of the buttress, left of *Central Crack.* Start on left side of buttress and make a rising traverse to the right until an exposed ledge is reached above the steep base of the buttress (140 ft.). The easiest line from here goes left, but make an exposed traverse back right onto the front of the buttress after 50 ft. Continue straight up, avoiding a steep wall on the right. Finish on the left of the great square wall where *Central Crack* enters from the right.

The Loch Avon Horseshoe: Carn Etchachan.—*Red Guard.*

R. Archbold & N. D. Keir. 29th May 1977. 850 ft. Severe.

This route follows an obvious line the full height of the cliff, between *Route Major* and *Scorpion*, commanding a fine position overlooking the entrance to *Castlegates Gully.* The presence of some vegetation may prove troublesome if wet. Evidence of earlier visitors was found.

Enter the gully (huge blocks), climb cracked slabs on the left to a good stance below a steep blank wall. On the left margin of the wall a chimney gives excellent climbing including two through routes to land in a grassy bay. The continuation fault looks dirty so move down and right into a groove (hidden hold). Follow the exposed groove which becomes more broken to the ledge system which traverses the cliff into *Scorpion.* Ahead is a steep cracked wall forming the left flank of a clean, wide, pink cracked shelf. Scramble rightwards along the ledge system until access is gained to the shelf. Climb it as far as a short corner on the right hand side leading up to a balcony stance atop the prominent, square cut overhang. Easier progress now as the cliff tilts back to meet the plateau.

M. Freeman & N. D. Keir. 24th March 1978. 10 hours. GRADE V.

In winter an excellent companion route to its neighbours. In the lower part, the soaring chimney was snow choked, but proved feasible using one of the through routes, the exit into the bay was awkward. Next, a tension traverse gained the groove, which required three pegs for aid (crux). Thereafter, the route continued to follow the summerline to the short corner leading off the pink cracked shelf in the upper part. Here the natural winter line was a snow covered ramp, round the profile, then directly up steep mixed ground to a cornice.

—The Sword. 950 ft. Grade V.
J. C. Higham & D. Wright. 5th March 1978. 7 hours.

This fine route follows a natural winter line up the buttress left of *False Scorpion Gully.* It crosses *Scorpion* just below the long chimney of that route, and takes the steep upper buttress by way of a tapering ramp. This ramp is the steep cracked shelf mentioned in the description of *Scorpion* and also partly climbed by the summer line of *Red Guard.* Start in a broken groove on the *Sentinel* just left of *Castlegates Gully.* On this ascent conditions forced a left traverse at 50 ft. into a chimney on the left, leading to the *Sentinel.* The buttress above the *Sentinel* was climbed more or less directly for 250 ft.; first by a long open groove, then by short, steep walls. A long, at first leftwards trending pitch led to the foot of the steep ramp. *Scorpion* crosses the route at this point. The ramp was climbed in two exposed pitches to its end, where a steep exit followed by a short traverse led to a large stance. An obvious groove and corner above led to a finish up convex snow slopes.

—Attic Rib. 300 ft. Grade III.
R. J. Archbold & D. M. Nichols. 5th March 1977.

The feature of this route is a steep, sinuous snow arête which forms towards the right hand end of the buttress, right of *Castle Gully.* Start leftwards up ramp, then move right and up a short step to gain left side of arête. Continue directly to cornice. On this ascent an awkward exit left was effected.

Shelter Stone Crag.*—Breach Gully.*
M. Freeman & G. S. Strange. 12th March 1977.   800 ft. Grade IV.

The prominent gully between *Castle Wall* and *Raeburn's Buttress.* The very steep blank section about 60 feet above the initial snow-bay was passed on the right and the gully regained above. An intriguing through-route followed by a traverse right led into the upper couloir. This was easy to the plateau.

Garbh Uisge Crag (the unnamed crag west of
Pinnacle Gully).—Blunderbuss. 450 ft. Grade III.
J. C. Higham & D. Wright. 4th March 1978.

The route follows the buttress bounding the left hand edge of *Garbh Gully* (see *S.M.C.J.*, 1977, xxxi, 173). Start at the foot of the buttress immediately on the left of *Garbh Gully.* The buttress is climbed directly, first by a steep chimney (150 ft.), then by a series of grooves and short walls, finishing by an open snow slope.

Hell's Lum Crag.*—Towering Inferno.*
R. Barton, A. Fyffe & E. Fyffe. 4th July 1977.   600 ft. Severe.

This route lies on the pillar left of *Brimstone Groove,* characterised by two rectangular roofs. Start directly below the pillar and climb straight up cracked green slabs for two pitches to gain the 'easy terraced fault' leading to *Deep Cut Chimney* (200 ft.). Climb the pink rock above moving left to gain a red vein; follow this into the corner leading to the lower roof, swing right onto the rib at the foot of this corner. Climb easy ground to peg belay in shallow chimney level with roof (140 ft.). Climb corner to below next overlap then move left onto the nose. Regain the fault and follow it to grassy recess (110 ft.). Continue up cracks and blocked walls to top (150 ft.). The first 200 ft. may be common with *Brimstone Groove.*

Variation—On pitch three, instead of moving left go straight up to small roof; cross it by a block to gain corner above. Climb corner, shallow inverted vee chimney, then rib to stance at top of original pitch three. (Very Severe).

—Devil Dancer.

R. Barton & A. Fyffe. 5th July 1977. 450 ft. Very Severe.

This route climbs the slabs between *Big De'il* and *Auld Nick*. Follow *Auld Nick* for two pitches to the belay below the roof. Continue over the bulge and overlaps via cracks then go left over the glacis to belay below a deep, left facing corner (70 ft.). Climb the corner, left at top, up a flake then belay in a deep recess at the left end of the long, low roof (80 ft.). Gain a horizontal flake, from its left end reach ledges on wall. Climb pink streak up and left to diagonal crack which leads to a ledge; go left into easy corner, belay above (100 ft.). Scramble to top.

The Stag Rocks: Longbow Crag.—*Windchill.*

R. Barton & A. Fyffe. July 1977. 530 ft. Very Severe.

This route follows a line between *Longbow Direct* and *Sand-Pyper*. The start of *Longbow Direct* (alternate start), is marked with a chipped arrow and 'G.S.' Start 15 ft. right of this, climb slab to diagonal overlap. Climb overlap on right and continue to stance and peg belay below shallow corner in next overlap (120 ft.). Traverse 15 ft. left to a left facing corner, climb it a short distance until possible to traverse awkwardly back right to a flake below a small roof. Continue slightly right to stance and peg belay below long, diagonal roof (shared with *Sand-Pyper*, 100 ft.). Climb roof on left, move down and left until fault and crack leads up and right to a ledge next to an arête. This is level with the large pitch five roof on *Sand-Pyper*. Peg belay (80 ft.). Move 20 ft. left to smooth recess by small natural arch. Climb recess into scoop above and up this until ledge leads right. Climb steep slab above into right facing groove which leads to juniper filled bay (100 ft.). Traverse right past blocks to gain groove with wide crack. Climb this and fine crack above to a good ledge (130 ft.). Move left into a chimney and scramble to top.

The following climb lies on the steep wall at the head of *Amphitheatre Gully*. It can be reached by a scramble down the broken ground above *Longbow Crag* and a traverse into the gully, or as an alternative finish to any of the routes on that crag.

—Amphitheatre Wall.

A. Fyffe & E. Fyffe. 13th August 1977. 200 ft. Hard Severe.

Climb the corner crack on the left of the wedge-shaped wall, to reach a grassy niche (100 ft.). Move up and right to gain a higher ledge and block belay (20 ft.). From the blocks step left and climb the crack over two dubious blocks to finish up a tapered chimney (80 ft.).

CAIRNGORMS II

Creagan a'Choire Etchachan: The Crimson Slabs.—*Scalpel.*

D. Dinwoodie & G. S. Strange. 11th July 1977. 300 ft. Hard Very Severe.

Takes the very shallow tilted groove between *Djibangi* and *Cutlass*. Climb the arête overlooking the initial grooves of *Cutlass* to belay ledge. Climb *Cutlass* for 30 ft. to small stance. Continue straight up the shallow groove for some 60 ft. to exit left on to small belay ledge. Above is a curving corner. Move left into another corner and climb this to join the curving corner higher up. Go up this and trend right to join *Djibangi*.

Ben Macdhui: Coire Sputan Dearg.—*Black Tower, Left-Hand Icefall.*

R. J. Archbold & D. M. Nichols. 6th March 1977.   300 ft. GRADE IV.

Difficulties were concentrated in the short, steep ice-filled groove, hard against the left wall of the *Black Tower*. After this, an easy snow gully led to the col behind the *Black Tower* summit. An attractive snow arête then led to the plateau.

Beinn a'Bhuird: Coire na Ciche.—*Hot Toddy.*   330 ft. Very Severe.

R. Archbold & N. D. Keir. 2nd July 1977.

Rearing up from *South Corner Gully* on its south wall before the fault fork of *Little Tower Gully*, and beyond *Sandy Crack*, is a well-defined, bulging headland. The following route takes a fairly direct line starting on the right hand side of an overhanging prow, and is recommended.

Climb shallow vertical fault tucked under prow, past a rock thread, and gain ledge on right (75 ft.). Step up and move left across undercut wall to layback up obvious crack (crux). Move up right and straddle over a rock bollard to good stance below overlap (75 ft.). Cross slab on right below overlap, up short grass trough to big ledge on brow of buttress (75 ft.). Climb slab and groove directly ahead leading to easy ground (120 ft.).

Garbh Choire.—*Gurkha.*   400 ft. Very Severe.

R. Archbold & N. D. Keir. 3rd July 1977.

The minor gully serving as an introduction to *Commando Route* provides a fine climb in its own right.

Go carefully up vegetatious rock to where a group of cracks strike up the left wall (120 ft.). Climb cracks onto rib giving access to higher bay immediately below overhanging cul-de-sac (75 ft.). Exit by the central slot, using one peg for aid (loose rock), gain key foothold on lip of overhang and so up to edge of slabs overlooking *Slochd Wall* (50 ft.). Climb obvious crack past knob of rock at steepening and continue straight up exposed right edge to rock peninsula at plateau (160 ft.).

On this occasion an expansive snowfield and a 12 ft. bergschrund posed unconventional difficulties of access.

CAIRNGORMS III

Coire Garbhlach.

This coire rises in two steps via a waterfall. The upper coire is bowl shaped and funnels into the gully described below. There was evidence of a huge avalanche previous to the first ascent.

—Waterfall Gully.   750 ft. GRADE III/IV.

E. Henderson + A. Douglas. November 1977.

Climb directly on the left of the waterfall to gain a rock gully (500 ft.). A steep ice pitch in the gully is climbed to reach an isolated rib of rock on the right (200 ft.). Continue to the lip of the coire, possible cornice finish (50 ft.).

The line of crags above the waterfall have provided excellent routes with some hard and exposed ice pitches. The total number of routes to date is six; all about 800-1,000 ft. long and of GRADE III/IV.

Upper Glen Feshie is framed between two crags: **Creag na Caillich** and Creag na Gaibhre. At the right hand end of Creag na Caillich is a prominent buttress flanked on the right by a large gully. This leads to a large crack at mid-height on the buttress. The following route climbs the gully and buttress.

—*Coylum Crack.*   1,000 ft. GRADE III/IV.

E. Henderson + A. Douglas. December 1977.

Climb the gully to reach the base of the buttress, reach the crack, keeping to the edge of the gully against the rock. From the crack traverse diagonally left to snow/rock shoulder then line of water runnel to top of buttress. An easy slope leads to shoulder of hill.

Facing Creag na Caillich is **Creag na Gaibhre**. The rocks are high up and divided by a waterfall. The following route climbs the waterfall.

—*Cascade Cave.*   250 ft. GRADE IV.

E. Henderson + A. Douglas. January 1978.

At the base of the waterfall is a large cave. Start at the cave and climb 100 ft. on rock to large ledge. Traverse right onto frozen waterfall. This gives exposed and severe ice climbing up to where overhang splits ice, take left fork and traverse diagonally to ice/rock shoulder then up spacious chimney to top.

Cairn Toul Braeriach: Garbh Coire Mór.—*White Nile.*

R. J. Archbold & M. Hillman. 12th March 1977.   400 ft. GRADE IV.

A continuous run of very steep ice between the middle and right hand buttresses of the *Pinnacles* trio. The route taken is obvious apart from a slight detour at two-thirds height, where one of the many ice walls encountered was avoided by a groove running diagonally left to an overlap, above which an iced slab allowed a traverse back right. No cornice difficulty on this ascent. Recommended.

CAIRNGORMS IV & V

Creag an Dubh Loch.—*Vertigo Wall.*   600 ft. GRADE V.

A. Nisbet & A. Robertson. 3rd-4th December 1977.

The route gave excellent mixed climbing and was both exposed and serious. The summer line was followed throughout using 8 points of aid (2 on the 'severe crack,' one for tension on the following traverse right, 2 ice screws in the 'wet chimney' where the ice was overhanging and rotten, and 3 on the steep wall after the 'creaking flake'). It is possible that a bolder ascent would eliminate all aid bar one in the severe crack and one on the summer crux. Due to limited daylight a planned but uncomfortable bivouac was made at half height. Most of the route is undercut and retreat from above the wet chimney would be difficult.

WESTERN HIGHLANDS

Ladhar Bheinn: Coire Dhorrcail: Spider Buttress.—*West Pillar.*

D. Dinwoodie & A. McIvor. 8th February 1978.   1,200 ft. GRADE III.

This is the right hand rib of *Spider Buttress* (see note by T. Patey in *S.M.C.J.*, 1963, xxvii, 373-374).

An icefall descends from the *Spider* snowfield. This was turned on the left by a snowpatch and easier grooves. A diagonal traverse across the *Spider* and up a snow ramp led onto the crest of the pillar, which was followed to the top.

—Face Route.

A. Nisbet & P. Tipton. 8th February 1978.   1,200 ft. GRADE III/IV.

This route climbs the face of the largest buttress; just left of *Viking Gully.* Climb into a prominent snow patch, aim for the top right hand corner, and climb the right hand of two grooves which lead to the buttress on the right near its top (*West Pillar*). An overhang at 200 ft. in the groove was turned on the right with a groove. Below the crest of the buttress an obvious left branch parallel to the buttress leads to the summit.

—Landlubbers Buttress.

A. Nisbet & P. Tipton. 9th February 1978.   800 ft. GRADE IV.

This is the sharp buttress in the centre of the coire, just right of *Raeburn's Gully.* Deceptively slabby but not sustained. The crux was a short, smooth slab which could bank out some winters. Climb the left side of the buttress to a rock band. Go to a prominent flake on the right skyline, pass it and go back left via snowy groove. Continue diagonally left past next rock band to reach snow ledge. A large block pinnacle can be seen above and slightly right. This was a cul-de-sac, so make a descending traverse left and cross the crux slab to reach an easy ramp which leads back to the crest of the buttress. Scramble to top.

Glen Strathfarrar: Coire Toll a Mhuic.

This large coire stretches from the east faces of Sgùrr na Muice and the south top of Sgùrr na Fearstaig. It is approximately one mile in length and access is by a two-mile stroll along a path. The road up Glen Strathfarrer is private; permission can be sought at the Post Office. The following routes are described under their respective summits.

Sgùrr na Muice: South East Face.—*Streaky.*

J. Mackenzie & J. Smith. 18th February 1978.   500 ft. GRADE III/IV.

On the approach this long face shows two parallel ice falls; this route climbs the thinner right hand fall nearest the edge. The long, curved couloir behind this face gives a good descent route.

Continuing past the nose of Sgùrr na Muice, the back wall of the coire appears and gives the following route:

—Trotter's Gully. 800 ft. GRADE III.

T. Anderson & J. Mackenzie. 19th February 1978.

Left of the col between the two peaks is a long curved gully within shallow walls. The left fork was finer and was climbed to a cornice finish. Descent by the col.

Sgùrr na Fearstaig: East Face.

The east face of this hill has a series of corners giving short routes at GRADE II/III standard.

Sgùrr na Lapaich: Garbh Choire: North East Face.—*Deer-Gran Gully.*

D. Langudge & J. Mackenzie. 25th February 1978.   400 ft. GRADE III.

A narrow east ridge falls from the summit; this route climbs a central line on the cliffs below the ridge.

CENTRAL HIGHLANDS

Creaǵ Dubh, Newtonmore: Waterfall Wall.—*Breakaway.*

200 ft. Hard Very Severe.

F. Allison & D. Cuthbertson. 11th September 1977.

Start at foot of steep wall just right of *Romp*. Climb wall by left hand groove to large block, step up above block then trend left to overlook tree filled groove. Continue up wall to ledge and belay (100 ft.). Move left and follow *Romp* for a few feet then follow break up and left to beneath roof. Turn roof on left on good holds and continue leftwards to finish up slab overlooking final groove of *Smirnoff.*

BEN NEVIS

Observatory Ridge: East Face.—*Silverside.*

380 ft. GRADE IV.

B. Dunn & D. Gardner. 17th April 1977.

Start 50 ft. below the original route on the east face (see *S.M.C.J.*, 1974, xxx, 276). Climb rightwards up snow and ice grooves to the left end of a large ledge. Traverse across left and climb round under a bulge to gain a line leading leftwards to a steep snow bay. Easier climbing now leads to the crest of the ridge.

Observatory Buttress.—*Rubicon Wall.*

400 ft. GRADE IV.

N. Muir & A. Paul. 14th April 1977.

Follows summer line approximately, in four pitches.

Central Trident Buttress.—*Cranium.*

300 ft. Very Severe.

N. Muir & A. Paul. 19th June 1977.

Climb large prominent crack left of *Metamorphosis* to gain cave at 70 ft. Exit via top of cave and climb steep wall leftwards as for *Heidbanger.* Belay on slab (80 ft.). Climb corner and wall to a doubtful flake, finish more easily (150 ft.). See photograph in *S.M.C.J.*, xxx, 1973, facing page 186.

GLENCOE, GLEN ETIVE & ARDGOUR

Buachaille Etive Mór: Coire na Tulaich: Creaǵ na Tulaich.

—*Easy Going.* 150 ft. Hard Very Severe.

D. Cuthbertson & M. Hamilton. 12th August 1977.

This short route climbs the left trending groove right of *Dwindle Wall*. Climb the groove and where it fades move left past a block to a small ledge. Climb shallow groove rightward to reach a shelf. Climb directly up short walls to top.

Bidean: Aonach Dubh: North Face.—*Massacre.*

A. Grigg & K. Johnstone. June 1977.   390 ft. Extremely Severe.

Start at the foot of *Tober.* Go up and right to niche below large, loose roof, climb roof and continue up left to ledge (60 ft.). Climb flake and awkward groove above, continue up to slanting crack and ledge (60 ft.). Follow crack up and left for 30 ft., pull over bulge and follow the Barrier Pitch of the *Girdle* for 40 ft. up and right. Climb mossy groove to ledge (130 ft.). Climb darker mossy corner above, move left to another corner and climb this to top (140 ft.). Four slings were used on the first ascent to facilitate gardening.

—Eldorado.

K. Johnstone & M. Worsley. June 1977.   330 ft. Extremely Severe.

Follows line left of *The Clearances* (see below). Start just right of crack, climb up and left into crack and follow this to ledge (nut for aid, 60 ft.). Follow groove to overhang, climb this by short corner and step left at top. Climb crack over smaller overhang (nut), go up and left to a ledge, and continue up crack to terrace (130 ft.). Last pitch as for *Massacre*.

—The Clearances.

E. Grindley, C. Grindley & J. Main. August 1976. 340 ft. Extremely Severe.

Start 20 ft. left of *Yo-Yo*. Climb slab leftwards below the obvious, thin crack on the left wall of *Yo-Yo*, move up and right across wall (peg runner in place), step right into crack and follow it to terrace (140 ft.). Climb corner above to the overhang, making a short excursion on the left wall, climb overhang (peg runner), continue to grass ledge (140 ft.). Continue more easily to top (60 ft.).

West Face: E. Buttress.—*Bannockburn.*

D. Cuthbertson & W. Todd. June 1977.   380 ft. Extremely Severe.

This supersedes *Tightrope*, as it frees the first pitch and finds an independent finish. Start as for *Trapeze*. Follow *Trapeze* for 20 ft. to a small ledge, step left to obvious flake crack. Climb this and traverse left along a break to a ledge halfway along pitch three of the *Big Top* (120 ft.). Climb wall above to terrace and belay (130 ft.). Above are two grooves, climb the left hand of these and finish by an easy groove (130 ft.). The right hand of the two grooves mentioned in the last pitch is the Direct Finish to *Trapeze*.

—Serenade.

K. Johnstone & M. Worsley. June 1977.   290 ft. Very Severe.

This follows a fairly obvious, left slanting line to the left of *Stickleback*. Start below left slanting break in overhangs. Climb slabby rock to reach obvious corner, climb corner (often wet), move right a few feet then follow obvious line up and left to belay in small niche on right wall (145 ft.). Step back left, follow ramp up left to arrive at hidden corner, climb corner and pull over roof at top (145 ft.).

F. Buttress.

The following two routes lie left and right of *Pocks* (see *S.M.C.J.*, 1966, xxviii, 224), on the clean, slabby wall across No. 4 Gully from the start of *Trapeze*.

—Nirvana.   160 ft. Very Severe.

C. Hill & D. N. Williams. 19th September 1976.

A grassy gully lies at the foot of the face. Start at the upper left of the face where the gully narrows. Climb up past a prominent cavity and gain ledge on right. Move right along the ledge and climb a crack which curves up and left to finish in a small bay directly above the start of the route (peg belay, 120 ft.). Scramble to top (40 ft.).

—Gazebo.   170 ft. Hard Very Severe.

C. Hill & D. N. Williams. 25th June 1977.

Gain the wall near the start of the grassy gully. Climb up and left until forced to make a long step right. Move up and back left to a ramp leading to a small ledge (2 nuts). Move across and then up to easier rocks. Belay in niche to the right of *Pocks* belay (3 pegs, 2 nuts, 130 ft.). Move up and left to finish up last few feet of *Pocks* (40 ft.).

East Face.—*The Fly.* 200 ft. Extremely Severe.

D. Cuthbertson & W. Todd. 9th July 1977.

Climbs the wall left of *Spider.* Start 30 ft. left of *Spider* at a crack. Climb this to ledge on right (40 ft.). Climb directly up wall above, move left into a scoop, go slightly left and up wall above to tree belay on terrace (100 ft.). Climb wall above (60 ft.).

—*Solitude.* 240 ft. Extremely Severe.

R. Anderson, D. Cuthbertson & W. Todd. 3rd June 1977.

Climbs wall right of *Spider.* Climb wall to ledge on *Spider* (30 ft.). From right end of ledge climb wall above directly, passing obvious block at 20 ft. (140 ft.). Finish up easy wall (70 ft.).

—*Quietude.* 200 ft. Very Severe.

D. Cuthbertson & W. Todd. 9th July 1977.

Start 50 ft. right of *Spider* below obvious overhang. Climb wall to ledge below overhang, climb overhang by left slanting crack to a ledge (80 ft.). Continue leftwards up wall above to shallow groove, climb this to terrace (80 ft.). Climb wall above (40 ft.).

—*Gambado.* 190 ft. Hard Very Severe.

R. Anderson, D. Cuthbertson & W. Todd. 3rd June 1977.

Start as for the old aid route *Dangle.* Climb first pitch of *Dangle* free, stepping left onto a ledge (50 ft.). Climb left trending fault through a bulge to a ledge (100 ft.). Finish up easy rocks (40 ft.).

Lower North-East Nose.—*Crocodile.*

250 ft. Extremely Severe.

W. Todd + R. Anderson, D. Cuthbertson & M. Hamilton. 4th/5th June 1977.

Start 20 ft. right of *Freak Out* at a left curving line of overhangs. Climb leftwards over the overhang to small ledge. Climb shallow groove above to ledge and belays of *Freak Out* (70 ft.). Climb groove on right for 20 ft., traverse right round corner to ledge below obvious groove (this pitch as for *Girdle,* 40 ft.). Climb groove, step left to ledge, climb edge above then finish more easily (140 ft.). See Glencoe notes.

SOUTHERN HIGHLANDS

Balnacoul Castle Crag: Glen Lednock: West Buttress.—*Chancers.*

E. Grindley & E. Brookes. June 1975. 150 ft. Extremely Severe.

This climb the overhanging corners and grooves just left of the *Great Crack.* (See *S.M.C.J.*, 1975, xxx, 390-392). Climb corner for about 60 ft .until level with a gangway on the left. Swing up right to the foot of a steep, thin corner crack. Climb this to a ledge and peg belay (100 ft.). Climb open corner above to the top of the prow and finish directly by a steep crack (50 ft.). (E. Grindley notes a free ascent of the *Great Crack,* May 1975).

Creag Tharsuinn.—*Tremolo.* 150 ft. Very Severe.

D. Dawson & W. Skidmore. 19th July 1977.

This short route lies on the steep wall left of *Tingler* (see *S.M.C.J.*, 1975, xxx, 392).

Start half-way up *Slab & Groove.* Traverse large flake right then follow thin crack up right. Climb crack over hard bulge moving left to belay on ledge (100 ft.). Move right, step off left end of flake and climb difficult wall to finish just left of *Tingler* (50 ft.).

Beinn a'Chreachain: North East Coire.—*The Circus*. 650 ft. GRADE III.
C. D. Grant & C. Stead. 16th January 1977.

This route lies on the main mass of rock in the left, or north-east corner of the coire. The crag is bounded on the left by a forked gully (GRADE I/II by right fork). Right of this is a prominent gully, slanting left to a central snow-field below a rockwall (GRADE II to the snowfield). Some 100 ft. right of this gully, and bounding the right hand side of the steepest part of the crag is an icefall. Climb the icefall to a ledge (150 ft.). Climb ice chimney to snowslope (150 ft.). Climb up leftwards by walls and grooves to the top.

Dunkeld: Craig-y-Barns: Cave Crag, Upper Tier.
—*Marjorie Razor Blade*. 100 ft. Extremely Severe.
D. Cuthbertson & M. Hamilton. 23rd February 1976.

Follows the S crack on the right wall of *Crutch*. Start between the cave and *Crutch*. Climb wall to ledge at foot of crack, climb crack (awkward), to ledge and belays (50 ft.). Traverse left and climb overhanging corner just right of *Crutch* to ledge and belays (30 ft.). Scramble to top (20 ft.).

Lover's Leap Crag.—*Jungle Jim*.
R. Baker & A. McCord. 3rd July 1977.   180 ft. Very Severe.

Start 50 ft. right of the corner of *Direct Route* at pointed rock. Climb wall directly to corner, follow corner to sloping wooded ledge, belay in corner below stunted holly. Climb to holly, move right and up groove exiting left into slabby bay. Continue diagonally rightwards to finish up heathery corner.

REGIONAL NOTES

Skye

Sgùrr MhicCoinnich: Coireachan Ruadha.—*Mongoose Direct*. On a visit in June 1977, P. Thomas & M. Fowler climbed the deep groove mentioned in the description of *Dawn Grooves*. From where the original route joins *Dawn Grooves*, instead of moving left onto the arête take the deep groove above, rejoining *Mongoose* higher when it re-enters the groove (150 ft., X.S.). (See *S.M.C.J.*, 1975, xxx, 383).

Coire Lagan: Sròn na Ciche.—*Atropos*. Hard Very Severe. Following a visit by M. Fowler & P. Thomas, this route, originally employing aid and somewhat circuitous route finding, is now free and direct. A description is amended. Climb the wall left of the original crack start, gain slab, follow crack to stance (65 ft.). Move up left through the overlap to gain an easy crack leading to the next overhang, climb this leftwards to a stance on the lip (100 ft.). Step right and climb the wall to easy ground (100 ft.).

Quiraing.—*The Needle*. 190 ft. Very Severe. We have a report of an ascent of the unclimbed *Needle* by K. & M. Bridges, starting up the east face and finishing on the north. They found the entire climb to be on loose, rotten and dangerous rock. Loose gear collectors might note that four abseil slings were left around the mound of grass and broken rock which constitutes the top.

Arran

Cioch na h'Oighe. The peg move on *Slipway* (see *S.M.C.J.*, 1976, xxxi, 52), which is very awkward, can be avoided by going up from the right hand edge of the ledge for ten feet then traversing left to step onto the ramp. The grade is unchanged at V.S. We thank W. Skidmore for this footnote.

Northern Highlands

Beinn Airigh Charr. W. D. Brooker supplies the following note. The location of *Square Buttress* is given incorrectly in both the Northern Highlands District and Rock Climbing guides. It lies S.W. (not E.) of 'the small unnamed lochan.' It is the prominent buttress left of the *Beanstalk* and forms the lower skyline as seen on the approach from Kearnsary. The new O.S. map allows precise location of some of the rock features hereabouts, viz.:—*Square Buttress*, 938765; **Martha's Peak:** *Eastern Lower Buttress*, 935767; *Main Face*, 932766.

The reference to a *Southern Buttress* in the District Guide is confusing since the summit of the mountain itself lies south of *Martha's Peak*. The two lower buttresses are rather like the parts of an arrowhead with the head formed by the main central face of *Martha's Peak*. The western lower buttress is of little interest but the eastern houses Slesser's *Lower Buttress Direct* and also featured in the 1909 ascent by Glover and Ling. In July 1977, A. G. Cousins and I climbed this *Lower Buttress*, starting at the lowest rocks and taking a natural line up the clean rocky crest defining its eastern edge. At about 400 ft., the steep wall which sweeps across the upper part of the buttress was breached by a pitch (50 ft., D.) leading shortly to the top of the *Lower Buttress*. (Slesser's route may lie further left). From here connection with the *Original Route* on the main face would require a rather contrived and far from easy traverse right. The continuation is by slabs, walls and ledges to the point where *Staircase Gully* runs out. Here it is easy if rather artificial to traverse right onto the upper part of the very steep main face and climb it to the summit. The whole climb gave a very enjoyable scramble, rather like a succession of curved ridges with the Difficult pitch the only point justifying the rope.

Applecross Group: Meall Gorm. At the entrance to the Bealach na Ba there is a very steep buttress on Meall Gorm (G.R. 795405) which is seen in profile from the hairpins. This was climbed by R. Archbold, G. S. Strange & K. .... in August 1977. The climbing which was mostly in grooves was steep, vegetated, loose and Very Severe.

Beinn Bhàn: Coire na Poite. R. J. Archbold & J. C. Higham note: 'We climbed the upper part of the upper connecting ridge of A'Poite (12th February 1978). The three steep tiers at the foot of the ridge were bare, and were avoided by climbing the main face at the back of Coire na Poite for about 450 ft. and then traversing right for another 450 ft. to the top of the third tier. The ridge was then followed for 700 ft. to the plateau. We understand that a similar ascent may have been done, but left unrecorded, a few years ago. However, it may be worth noting that for length, variety and scenery, we found this to be one of the finest GRADE III climbs in the country.'

The Editor notes the somewhat confused state of data on this area, and would like to comment that like any other calculating machine the correct answers will only be given out if adequate correct information is supplied in the first instance. Rumour has it that K. Spence has climbed a GRADE V icefall in Coire na Poite, but like D. Lang in an earlier issue of the *Journal*, we are tired of rumours, and would view with sympathy ascents sent in.

Beinn Eight: Coire Mhic Fhearchair.—*The Tower Direct.* D. M. Nichols notes that after an awkward start the steep centre face of *The Tower* gives a pleasant route at Difficult standard, useful for access to the *Central Wall* (April 1976).

Foinaven: Cnoc a' Mhadaidh (G.R. 528327). D. Butterworth & D. McCallum (October 1977), note an ascent of a 350 ft. Severe. The route is difficult to find owing to vegetation, but for the hortophiliac it lies north of the main crag, 100 yards north-east of the large gully separating the two.

Cairngorms

Carn Etchachan. R. J. Archbold sends a list of corrections for this crag, particularly relating to the area between *False Scorpion* and *Castlegates Gully* where there is much confusion. We hope to publish an up-dating of this crag in the next issue.

Choire Etchachan: *Bodkin.* Winter ascent, GRADE IV. D. Renshaw & G. S. Strange, 30th January 1977.

Beinn a Bhuird, Garbh Choire: *Mitre Ridge.—Original Route.* Winter ascent of the direct start by W. S. McKerrow & D. M. Nichols, 26th March 1977. Climbed on good snow, the overlap in the middle was taken at its lowest by groove on the right.

Cumming Crofton Route. Winter ascent, GRADE V. D. Renshaw & G. S. Strange, 26th February 1977.

Stob an t'Sluichd.—*Pinnacle Ridge.* Winter ascent, GRADE III. M. Freeman & G. S. Strange, 11th April 1977.

Coire An Dubh Lochain.—*Polypody Groove—Variation.* From the point about 250 ft. up where the route moves out of the groove and up to a ledge on the left, an alternative to turning the steep section above on the left is to regain the groove by a delicate slant to the right (Severe).

Creag An Dubh Loch.—*The Giant.* This is now completely free, D. Cuthbertson & M. Hamilton taking the original line in June 1977. *Cougar* was also freed by the same team in June 1977, the original route was followed except for the last pitch, a description of which is amended:—'Make the mantelshelf onto the block, climb crack with protruding stone to reach overlap. Make left traverse to reach good rounded spike, step up and traverse left passing old peg (crux), continue leftwards until possible to move up and and left to ledge belay under roof (150 ft.). Scramble to top.'

A. Nisbet notes:—'On the second (?) winter ascent of *False Gully*, the chimney of the summer and original winter line looked unaccommodating and a variation was made. Following a hard move round a corner on the ledge beyond the chimney, a tension traverse was made across a smooth slab to snow ledges. We were then forced to climb diagonally leftwards to finish near the top of *King Rat*. The tension traverse may go with good ice.'

W. Todd notes a free ascent of *Falkenhorst* at X.S., in company with A. Last.

Lochnagar.—*Giant's Head Direct.* A. Nisbet notes: 'Early ascents of this route involved climbing an icy ramp on the left of the chimney to gain the upper (direct) section. The ice on the ramp does not form every year, and the last two ascents have climbed instead up to the overhanging barrier keeping slightly right, stepping left immediately under it. The quality and difficulty of the route is confirmed.'

—The Cathedral. Winter ascent, GRADE III, by the obvious deep chimney near the right hand end of the buttress. M. Freeman & G. S. Strange, 12th December 1977.

Ben Nevis

Titan's Wall. This was freed in June 1977 by M. Fowler & P. Thomas, the original aid line being climbed at Extremely Severe. Four days later, on the second free ascent, D. Cuthbertson & M. Hamilton climbed the route with a slight variation, finishing more directly via an awkward 30 ft. crack. This route must now rate as one of the most difficult on the hill.

Glencoe

Bidean: Aonach Dubh: Lower North East Nose.—*Freak Out.* Extremely Severe. Following an unseemly period after the first ascent 11 years ago, we note with satisfaction a recent ascent by D. Cuthbertson reducing the original 20 points of aid down to one lonely peg. An up-to-date description follows:

The route climbs the obvious crack in the pink wall right of *Boomerang.* Scramble up the lowest rocks to ledge with flake and tree belay below crack. (30 ft.). Climb wall to gain crack, follow crack until right traverse leads to small ledge with old peg and nut belays (75 ft.). Traverse back left to main crack line, climb crack to roof, pull over this on good hold then reach up and right for peg (in situ). Using peg gain better section of crack, continue up crack then trend leftwards heading for a down pointing flake. Using flake gain resting position under final roof. Climb roof rightwards until possible to pull out onto ledge step left to belay (100 ft.). Climb wall above to top (50 ft.).

Buachaille Etive Mór: East Face, North Buttress.—*Bogtrotter* was free climbed by K. Johnstone & W. Todd and is now harder at X.S. and just as unappealing as before.

The Etive Slabs.—*Swastika.* The top pitch was free climbed by M. Hamilton & W. Todd at X.S. While always happy, and occasionally even impressed to see some routes freed, this might be a case where the majority would still prefer swinging about in slings after smoothing up the slabs below.

Southern Highlands

Creag Tharsuinn. W. Skidmore reports the following improvements to routes on this hill, and contrary to rumour, would like to point out that none of these activities have any connection with any Job Creation Scheme.

—*Terminal Wall.* The second pitch should now read 'climb left wall to groove with flakes, leave on left and climb to crack and groove left of second overhang. Traverse hard left from bottom of crack to gain main crack line which follow over sentry box and bulges to small ledge high on face . . . .'

—*Tingler.* The last pitch should read 'climb wide crack above belay, swing left round edge (same point can be gained by direct ascent of front face—Hard), and climb straight up via flake to top. Peg belay (in place) on edge. We can confirm the interest of *The Tingler,* and add that *Terminal Wall* looks very good. For descriptions of these routes see *S.M.C.J.*'s 1976, xxxi, 59 and 1975, xxx, 392 respectively.

Glen Kinglass. J. Mackenzie supplies the following notes on a crag which has been climbed on before but shortage of information prompts us to say a little more. The rocks lie on **Binnean an Fhidleir** (2,680 ft. point), about ⅔ mile north east of the summit, and can be approached via Glen Kinglas taking the path as far as Abyssinia bothy. A walk of about 1,200 ft. takes one to the cliffs, following a stream. The rocks are in three parts: a 250 ft., central wall, with slabs on either side. The rock is sound schist, rougher than the *Cobbler* variety with an easily removed black moss. Five routes were described, but we will leave the crags for exploration, and possible future maturation.

Creag Liath. K. Schwartz notes several short routes on this crag. These include a 90 ft. Very Difficult climbing the right hand of two diédres right and below *Wedlock,* and a 120 ft. Hard Very Severe, *Canaille,* climbing the first pitch of *Apex Groove* then two corners above. Both these were climbed with R. Schwartz in June 1977.

Outcrops

Dumbarton Rock. We note free ascents of *Snow White*, the 60 ft. crack line left of the *Hustler* (W. Todd), and *The Big Zipper*, after the initial two bolts (M. Hamilton). The grades were Hard Very Severe and Extremely Severe respectively.

Craig-y-Barns.—*Rat Race* has now been freed by M. Hamilton at Extremely Severe. Repeat ascents of *Rat Race, Squirm Direct* and *Corpse* confirm their technical interests.

LETTER TO THE EDITOR

Sir—The alphabetical rule for route-makers has now been in operation for nearly ten years and seems to have received fairly general approval. Seconds certainly like it, as do those with surnames from A to M and I can't say I haven't benefited from time to time on both counts. Others have had to choose their partners more carefully! But to be serious, I believe the system to be a healthy one in that it gives credit to teams rather than to individual climbers; and it is interesting to note how few of your contributors have felt it necessary to add the permitted designation 'ldr' after the leader's name. The second man's competence has a relevance on the Ben which it does not have on, say a gritstone edge and the system is obviously appropriate in Scotland in a way that it would never be in the more purely gymnastic climbing areas.

The algebraic notation proposed in last year's *Journal* represents something rather worse than a return to the old system. It provides for easy identification not only of the leader in a rope of two but of the straggler in ropes of three or more, 'where the information is available.' Evidently therefore we are now inviting this information and by doing so I fear we are encouraging glory-seekers in a way we have never done before. Even south of the Border, the practice is still to draw attention to notable 'alternate leads' rather than to notable leads. Do we want a more competitive climbing scene here than there? At best, the proposed new system will lead only to a confused historical picture, especially if the information is later transferred to guide-books. Readers will then have to consider during which New Route Editor's reign a first ascent took place before deciding what relevance, if any, is to be attached to the order of the pioneers' names and to the presence or absence of the hieroglyphics.

I propose that the alphabetical system should be restored without 'ldr's or plus signs and that all descriptions in future guide-books be altered accordingly. As we have been told before, those who wish to blow their trumpets or to castigate their seconds can always do so by writing articles for the *Journal*! In any case, before we go any further let us sound out members' views and try to decide upon a reasonably permanent policy for the future. Yours etc.

PETER F. MACDONALD.

MISCELLANEOUS NOTES

Mountain Bothies Association Sourlies Project.—In these days of soaring costs and the apparent attitude of 'Think of a Number and then Double it,' it is both instructive and refreshing to see such a worthwhile result from such a small financial expenditure. We therefore print the full report on this project including the accounts. It was sent to us by the project organiser, David Dixon, who we hope one day will be our Chancellor of the Exchequer.

'The Scottish Mountaineering Trust donated £150 towards the rebuilding of the byre at Sourlies to provide an open shelter in accordance with the aims of the Association. The site is at the head of Loch Nevis on land owned by Knoydart Estate from whom permission had been obtained for the renovation.

'The work was carried out over the period 15th-22nd April, 1977. Local timber was cut by the estate sawmill at Inverie and ferried up the loch on the Friday (15th) afternoon. It had been arranged for further materials, tools, equipment and volunteers to be ferried in on the Saturday morning but due to the different type of boat and the state of the tide, everything was dumped on the North Morar shore about a mile from the bothy in heavy rain with the rivers in spate! In spite of these difficulties, by late afternoon most of the equipment had arrived on site and work started.

'The project entailed the building in stone of a half-gable window facing N.W., complete roof frame, sarking and sheeting together with the construction of a fireplace and 10 ft high chimney stack also in dry stone with flue liners inside. A small window was put in the back of the bothy and the very wide doorway converted into a fixed window and narrower door. This provides a fine view of the loch and with two clear panels in the roof, the interior is fairly light. A sleeping platform, benches and a table were made and four metal chairs brought in so that comforts are not entirely lacking. The outside walls were largely left 'dry' to maintain the original appearance but the inside walls were pointed up with cement to cut out draughts.

'Stone was taken from the ruins of the old house at Sourlies (the last house to be inhabited at the head of the loch) and sand was obtained locally. An improvement on previous projects was made by putting sarking on the roof to cut out condensation and a new method of sealing the roof at the gables was used which it is felt will also be an improvement and successfully resist the westerly gales.

'The 10 persons involved in the main work party were hard pressed when further heavy rain towards the end of the week hampered progress but everything was sealed up by the Thursday night and the bothy duly opened on the Friday morning (22nd April) by Mr George Cheyne, Chairman of the Scottish Rights of Way Society Ltd., who, with his wife, braved the torrential rain to come out with the estate boat to uplift a sodden but still happy work party. We took with us many memories of the place bathed in spring sunshine (as well as rain!) and left behind a shelter which we hope will be of benefit to others exploring this fine area.

ACCOUNTS

Expenditurre				Income		
Roof sheeting			£95·49	Grant (S.M.T.)		£150·00
Two clear roof panels			10·95	Donation (Scottish Rights		
Timber for roof			182·80	of Way Society)		100·00
Boat hire			71·28	Donation (St. Andrews		
Ridge board			9·00	University		
Door frame and perspex			10·32	Mountaineering Club)		30·40
Nails			4·00	Donations—various		
Paint			2·89	personal		49·60
Cement			15·27	Allocation from M.B.A.		
Roofing felt			2·50	funds		85·00
Cuprinol			10·50			
	Total	£415·00				£415·00

Perspex for windows, timber for the sleeping platform, aluminium ridge irons, drive screws, roofing nails and various sundries were drawn from M.B.A. Stocks.'

On the Knees of the Gods.—This year Geoff Cohen, with Gordon Macnair and Dave Broadhead repeated the winter traverse of the Cuillin, originally described in *S.M.C.J.*, xxviii, 1965. Cohen sends us an account of this splendid expedition:

Tom Patey described the winter traverse of the Cuillin Ridge as 'the greatest single adventure in British mountaineering.' I cannot but agree with him and would even go so far as to say that there can be few outings of comparable length anywhere to surpass it for sheer beauty, variety and mountaineering enjoyment. Without being technically difficult the climbing is always interesting and the situations incomparably fine. For me it was undoubtedly the expedition of a lifetime and I only wish I could do justice to it as wittily as Tom Patey.

We arrived at Sligachan early on Friday, 10th February, unable to believe our luck at finding Sgùrr nan Gillean draped in white and glistening in the morning sun. We treated the ridge like a fairly serious Alpine route, taking several days' food and plenty of bivvy gear. This was just as well for the nights were as cold as any we could remember in the Alps or elsewhere. Even our oranges froze in the middle. We set out about mid-day and took the ordinary route up the West ridge of Sgùrr nan Gillean, getting to the top about 3 o'clock. The main ridge was absolutely plastered, not just with a light cover, but with a thick consolidated cover of good snow. Only in a few places further on did we encounter quite dangerous windslab, the most alarming occasion being when a piece about 50 feet square swished off just below us. At first we climbed a bit cautiously, not being quite sure how well the snow was adhering on the steeper sections, but we soon got into the swing of it and soloed the vast majority of the route, only roping up for one or two pitches. The abseils were probably the most dramatic parts of the ridge, particularly down *Naismith's Route* and *King's Chimney*.

On the first day we just got down the Bhasteir Tooth as daylight was fading and found an excellent bivvy site on the Bealach na Lice between two large boulders. The second day gave some interesting climbing and a few tricky descents on Bidein Druim nan Ramh and Sgùrr a Mhadaidh. After Mhadaidh there was a delightful section of ridge, really narrow but encrusted with excellent snow. Our second bivvy was just below the Inaccessible Pinnacle, about 100 feet down the slope. We woke to another brilliant day on the 12th and had a go at the East ridge of the Inaccessible Pinnacle. It was an amazing sight, with the Coruisk side and the East ridge plastered in ice and hoar while the Coire Lagan side was completely bare. Despite the sun there was a strong cold wind coming from the south-east and unfortunately finding holds under the thick hoar was rather time-consuming. Having got up about 70 feet to a level section we decided that although the remainder looked less steep lack of time would not allow us to complete the route, and so we abseiled off. We carried on straight down the ridge of An Stac in two abseils and then easily up to Mhic Choinnich. The abseil down *King's Chimney* was really exciting—first trying to excavate a block while poised, in a strong wind, on an exposed slope of hard nevé, and then coming down the right wall of the corner which was encased in an enormous sheet of ice. The climb up to Thearlaich looked tricky but was quite reasonable, and the descent off it gave some pleasant climbing of about V.D. standard. To save time we missed out Sgùrr Alasdair and got to grips with the *T. D. Gap*. Our lassoing attempts from the gap were unsuccessful, so we just went down the gully on the Coir a Ghrunnda side and rejoined the ridge beyond. This did not seem much of a detour and I doubt if it lost us any time. We were rewarded for our time saving efforts by a superb sunset behind the outer isles as we climbed up to Garsbheinn. With story book timing we reached the summit just as the sun dipped into the sea. Even then our feast of views was not quite over—as we slipped along the icy path back to Glenbrittle the moon came out to give us a wonderful reflection from the waters of Loch Brittle.

April, 1977   *Photos: David Dixon*

Sourlies Bothy—Before and After

The Easter Meet—Braemar, 1977

Photo: Fiona Donaldson

Guest, J. R. Marshall, T. Nicolson, Guest, O. Turnbull

M. H. Cooke

N. Ledingham, C. Elton (guest), R. Elton, R. C. S. Lowe, R. G. Folkard, H. H. Mills

W. McKenzie, B. Fraser, K. Macrae   W. T. Taylor, G. S. Roger, C. C. Gorrie

J. C. Donaldson, D. J. Bennet   C. B. M. Warren

Mur Gorm Tir nan Og.—One of our younger members who happens to have been alive for seventy years completed the traverse of the Cuillin Ridge last year. Charles Warren did the traverse starting at the seaward end and ending approximately at Sgùrr nan Gillean.

The Glen Shiel Circuit.—Blyth Wright sends us this note about an attempt he made in July, 1977, to complete all the Munros on either side of Glen Shiel during a 24 hour period. It was a venture in the same spirit as the Glen Nevis circuit which he tried with Philip Tranter in 1964 and which Tranter completed:

'Leaving Glenmore Lodge about 4 a.m. on the 14th, I drove to Glen Shiel and left my motor bike at Mhalagain bridge at 6.25 a.m. I reached the summit of Sgùrr Fhuaran at 8.40 a.m. and, traversing the main ridge eastwards, arrived on Ciste Dhubh at 1.09 p.m. Descending to An Caorann Mór, I continued eastwards over Mullach Fraoch-Choire, A'Chralaig, Sgùrr nan Conbhairean and Càrn Ghluasaid, which I reached at 6.27 p.m. For reasons which seemed good at the time I by-passed Tigh Mór. I then descended to the main road and turned back westwards reached the hotel at Cluanie at 8.15 p.m.

'After some very welcome refreshment, I left again at 8.50 p.m. and reached the summit of Druim Shionnach at 10.42. After a diversion to Creag a Mhaim (11.13 p.m.) at the east end of the S. Cluanie ridge, I came back over Druim Shionnach and traversed the ridge westwards to Creag nam Damh, arriving there at 4.25 a.m. on the 15th. Here it became obvious that I would not have enough time to continue to Sgùrr na Sgine and the Saddle without exceeding my 24 hour limit, so I descended to Mhalagain, arriving there at 5.56 a.m. Some time later, I remounted my bike and drove back to Glenmore Lodge, arriving about 11.45 a.m.

'Obviously, I did not succeed in my main intention of climbing all the Cluanie Munros, managing only 17 out of the 20, but I still found it interesting to compare the figures with those of the Nevis circuit. The latter comprises about 6,050 metres of ascent and 52.5 kilometers of distance (i.e. 32.5 miles and not 36 as we believed at the time). The figures for the Cluanie circuit are 5,720 metres and 59.5 kilometres respectively. By Naismith, this makes the Cluanie trip about 50 minutes more strenuous, although the Nevis circuit embraces one more Munro, at 18. The opportunity obviously exists for a strong walker to make the complete Cluanie circuit, thus firmly establishing its pre-eminence! More sensible use of the daylight available would in itself make this possible.

D'ye ken Glen Coe.—The new edition of the Glen Coe Guide will be under the typekeys this autumn. Any relevant information will be most welcome and should be sent to the New Routes Editor, address at back of the *Journal*. Additionally, black and white prints of climbers in action in Glen Coe will be looked at (but regretfully not returned) with a view to publication in the forthcoming guide. We will pay 70-80 Zloty for any print used. If your favourite route is not included in the new guide it may be your fault.

Hark the Herald.—In a previous *Journal* (*S.M.C.J.*, 1975, xxx, 405) we suggested that we might appoint a Lord Lyon who would scrutinise the credentials of those who claim to have completed the Munros and who, when satisfied, would award the appropriate Heraldic Achievements. Then again, it might be more appropriate to adopt a process similar to canonisation, the applicant passing through carefully scrutinised stages until the full triune sanctity of Munrohood (the real ones, the tops and the furth) is achieved, a state usually recognisable by the authentic odour of sweat that surrounds the candidate. Then, there is the difficult case of Hamish Brown's dog (*S.M.C.J.*, 1972, xxx, 87)—does it qualify for a number or not? Are all mammals eligible for Munrohood? If so, the Brownian hound may just squeak in to the First Hundred as the centennial portcullis seems to fall just about its tail. In so doing it would push out some *H. sapiens* or other from membership of the Elect. Is this tolerable? Moreover, according to usually well-informed sources the dog has caused other trouble. It almost precipitated an accident after its ascent of the Inaccessible Pinnacle; a hard man heaving himself up onto the summit platform from *Varicose* almost fell off when his emerging face was greeted with a cheerful woof and a lick from the welcoming dog who had pipped him at the post. More prosaically, the Editor has received a letter from an earnest reader suggesting a MUNROISTS' TIE be instituted. This would not be as good as a shield, properly quartered and hung over the owner's place at the *Club* dinner, but it might do to be going on with. We, therefore, invite designs for such an article from all sorts of interested persons. The response, if any, will be fully reported in next year's *Journal*. Who knows, the winning design may even merit honorary Munrohood (or bar) for its perpetrator!

Sisyphus Unchained.—The following Munroists seem to have rolled their stones onto the last Cairn and now lie uneasily on their laurels as they wait for the next move by their cunning adversaries. You would have to be fell naive to think that the Munros have had their last skirmish with the Ordnance Survey whose leg they have been pulling mercilessly in the last few years. Mountains that are able to change their map references as well as their heights (*S.M.C.J.*, xxx, 1975, 403) and even acquire complex new names (for Gaelic is still spoken among the hills) are not going to be pinned down for all time by little men with theodolites, or laser beams or whatever the surveying cognoscenti are currently using to catalogue every kaim and kettle of its Kingdom. Anyway, three hearty pechs for the following:

(144) Campbell R. Steven, 1976, —, —;   (152) M. H. MacKinnon, 1977, —, —;
(145) R. Davie, 1976, —, —;   (153) Denise Marsden, 1977, 1977,
(146) Erland Flett, 1977, —, —;   —;
(147) A. N. Darbyshire, 1977, —, —;   (154) W. M. Donaldson, 1977, —, —;
(148) Jock Murray, 1977, —, —;   (155) Duncan C. Gray, 1978, —, —;
(149) Edward F. Emley, 1977, —, —;   (156) Iain G. Gray, 1978, —, —;
(150) R. D. Leitch, 1977, —, —;   (157) Miss D. S. Annonymous, 1977,
(151) W. Myles, 1977, —, —;   —, —;

(154) Bill Donaldson was accompanied on his final ascent by two pipers whose names are recorded as D. McLeod and B. Fleming and by W. MacKenzie, a senior and kenspeckle dignitary of the Club.

(149) E. F. Emley records that his long march took 40 years and expressed a feeling of relief as he can now turn to lower mountains of character and enjoy the charms of Baosbheinn and Beinn Airidh Charr without feeling he should be trudging on through dub and mire to some featureless Munro because it's there.

There was an outbreak of champagne drinking on Ben More, Mull when (131) C. Marsden arrived on the top with the brand new (153) Denise Marsden. There is also a coy note on one piece of paper in this year's file which just says 'Miss D. S. Annonymous' (sic) probably a relative of the well-known poet. Should this coy mistress be included? Why not? Why restrict the accolade to the brazen? The criteria for admission to the Munrobility as readers of the previous paragraph will have realised are dogged with problems like this. (156) I Gray and (155) D. Gray are father and son (the first (?) father/son combination with the same spirit in this field at any rate).

The following, formerly blessed, have now achieved the full trinity:

(117) A. E. Lawson, 1974, 1974, 1976   (139) R. Morgan, 1976, 1976, 1977. There is also a note to say that (92) R. Hainsworth should read 1969, 1969— and not 1973, 1973—which should be the appendage of (84) R. Cook, the two having been transposed accidentally in *S.M.C.J.*, 1976, xxxi, 65. Also (114) J. Dawson should be 1973, 1973—and not merely 1973, —, as reported in *S.M.C.J.*, 1975, xxx, 405.

You see what we mean about the need for a full-time Lord Lyon? Maybe it would be better if we just hung and drew these people without any quarter.

More Revisionist Tendencies.—The O.S. Second Series Maps are unlikely to be finally completed for another ten years. After Sheet 42 (Rannoch), due out next year, a sizeable chunk of the Southern Highlands will remain unrevised until later. However, we hope that the Ordnance Survey can be persuaded to divulge some of its secrets in advance of map publication to allow new and definitive Munros Tables and accompanying guidebooks to be published. This will be a major revision and hopefully (the Survey resting on its orogenetic laurels for a bit) a long lasting one. If Munroists, Compleat or Aspirant, or even ordinary mortals, have strong feelings as to any promotions, demotions or other changes they would like to see in the final work, they should express these to either Jim Donaldson or Hamish Brown who are the joint arbiters and authors.

Big White Woofers.—Avalanches appear to be increasingly evident among accident causes in Scotland during recent years. While the growth in numbers of people abroad in the winter hills has contributed to this, the big late snowfalls of the last two winters have certainly led to frequent and often spectacular avalanches being observed. During a visit to the Shelter Stone in April this year avalanches were heard coming down through the night and one of these was found next day to have swept the slope below Hell's Lum Crag for over 500 yards on a broad front. The factors governing avalanche release in Scotland differ from those applicable in the Alps and are far from being fully understood. Studies are now being carried out and it would be of great assistance to this research if as many Scottish avalanches as possible are recorded. It would be appreciated if anyone observing an avalanche or recent remains would send details such as location, time, size, type, etc., to *Rod Ward, Department of Geography, University of Aberdeen.*

SCOTTISH MOUNTAIN ACCIDENTS, 1977

IN THE PAST the accident reports have come from Ben Humble who left his own characteristic imprint upon the annual accident survey. Adherents to tradition will be pleased to see that the *simple slip* has survived its progenitor.

To follow in Ben's redoubtable steps is no sinecure and we welcome Raymond Sefton who has taken on this particular M.R.C.S. responsibility, and wish him well in the difficult task of compiling the report. Ray will be known to some members as the former leader of the R.A.F. Leuchars team.

As usual we express our indebtedness to the M.R.C.S. for the information below and record appreciation of the varied efforts of the Mountain Rescue services.

M.R.C.S. Accident Survey 1977

The total number of incidents has increased during 1977, but no conclusion should be drawn from this.

Many of the incidents are of a minor nature, but nevertheless have initiated a Call Out and used the resources of the rescue services.

Once again the majority of accidents are caused by simple slips when hill walking in both summer and winter. What does appear significant is the relatively small number of climbers who get into difficulty, once they have roped up and started to climb. Most of their problems seem to come in the approach or the descent after a climb is completed.

Apart from Tourists, the standard of equipment being carried by most people on the mountains is good. This can be seen from those who are benighted and turn up the next day with no harmful effects.

The Table attempts to show the primary causes of mountain accidents. However, any incident can be caused by a combination of factors. For example: a report showing a benightment could in fact be caused by a navigational error. On many occasions the incident is caused by loss of a map or separation. Ideally, each member of a party should carry a map and compass.

1977 STATISTICS

Category	Dead	Injured	Casualties Uninjured	Missing	Total
Hill Walking	7	41	51	—	100
Climbing	7	14	10	—	31
Ski-ing	2	—	5	—	7
Miscellaneous	4	3	14	2	23
TOTAL	20	58	80	2	161

Miscellaneous includes incidents to Locals, Estate Workers, etc.

There were a total of 135 M.R. Team Call Outs, 19 involving S.A.R.D.A. dogs and 26 searches.

R.A.F. helicopters were used on 65 occasions.

CAUSES OF INCIDENTS

Cause	Number	Cause	Number
Illness	8	Falls, Winter Climbing (unroped)	5
Navigation Errors	4	Falls through Cornice	2
Separation	6	Glissading	4
Poor Timing	5	Avalanche	4
Benightment	10	Cragfast	3
False Alarms	7	Rock Fall	2
Slips on rock/scree, Hillwalking	26	Abseiling	2
Slips on ice/snow, Hillwalking	10	Non-Mountaineering	5
Falls on rock (roped)	2	Lightning Strike	1
Falls on rock (unroped)	2	Exhaustion/Exposure	13
Falls, Winter Climbing (roped)	2		

These are the basic causes of the incidents. In many cases a combination of causes may be responsible for the incident.

Accident List

This omits incidents not connected with hillwalking or mountaineering.

CAIRNGORMS

JANUARY 8—Whilst descending Central Couloir Coire an Lochain, a climber tripped and rolled 200 feet, injuring his ankle.

JANUARY 12—In bad weather a party became overdue between Ben Macdui and Cairngorm Car Park.

JANUARY 22—Three schoolboys were taking part in the Duke of Edinburgh's Silver Award expedition near Braemar. About 6 p.m., on Friday, 21st January, 1977, the three boys were driven to a car park near Glenshee Chairlift by one of their schoolmasters from where they were to start their expedition. The boys made their way on foot to a disused hut about a mile away on the side of Meall Odhar where they spent a cold, miserable night. Their intended route was Càrn Aosda, The Cairnwell, An Socach, Càrn a Gheòidh and thereafter to Gulabin Lodge. They set off at 8 a.m., and on reaching the summit of Càrn Aosda decided to miss out the Cairnwell because it was hard going in soft, wet snow and make straight for An Socach. About 2 p.m., they were about 400 feet from the summit when one of them collapsed. His two companions went to his aid and after erecting a tent over him gave him coffee. They changed his wet clothing and put him in a sleeping bag. He was evacuated with exposure.

MARCH 4—A climber fell and broke his femur on the great slab Coire an Lochain.

MARCH 6—Climber overbalanced whilst retrieving rope after an abseil on Red Craig, Glen Clova. Sustained broken pelvis.

MARCH 12—Two experienced skiers ski-ing round the four tops were delayed due to unsuitable ski conditions. Got lost in the Lairig Ghru, abandoned their skis and eventually turned up unharmed at 1.00 a.m.

MARCH 13—Whilst sitting down to lunch on the snow in Coire an Lochain a climber slipped, failed to hold his axe and fell injuring his pelvis.

MARCH 23—A group of hill walkers found an unused tent about 1 mile south of Bynack Lodge. The police eventually traced the owner who had abandoned it in bad weather and not reported it.

MARCH 29—An experienced party of walkers going from Glenmore to Macdui and back via Strathnethy were overdue.

APRIL 6—A man stepped through a cornice on top of Cairn Lochan. Survived a fall to the bottom and walked out.

APRIL 6—A climber soloing Parallel Gully 'A', Lochnagar, on ice, fell 200 feet and was critically injured.

MAY 8—A family of four were directed to walk onto the Lairig Ghru, through the Chalamain Gap and back to Aviemore. They were advised to stay off the tops due to snow showers. They had no map or compass and were poorly equipped. They got into the Lairig, but due to wind and zero navigation ability ended up going left across the shoulder of Càrn a'Mhaim and then to Derry. They had no idea of their predicament. The party were cold, wet and exhausted when they arrived about an hour before darkness.

MAY 21—A party of relatively inexperienced walkers set off from Aviemore to walk through the Lairig Ghru to Braemar. Near Corrour one of them injured his foot. At Am Pros na Meearlich they missed the ford over the Luibeg and continued down the right bank of the stream to Luibeg Cottage. They were unable to continue and had to be picked up by Landrover.

MAY 21—A hillwalker suffered a coronary thrombosis on the ridge between Dubh Loch and Loch Buidhe and died.

JUNE 24—A hill walker fell and broke a leg on the east side of Srón na Lairig.

JULY 9—A boy fell on the Fiacaill of Coire-an-t-Sneachda and suffered head and back injuries.

JULY 17—A 16-year-old boy suffering from blisters and fatigue became separated from his two companions about half a mile north of the Sinclair Hut. The two leading boys made their way to Aviemore via the Iron Bridge. Here they met a south-bound walker and asked him to tell the slower boy that they would be camping in Aviemore. Meanwhile, their friend arrived in Aviemore via Rothiemurchus Lodge. When the three did not meet up, a search was initiated.

JULY 23—Two climbers set out to climb *Mousetrap*, Creag an Dubh Loch at 4 p.m. They seriously misjudged conditions and completed the climb at 10.30 p.m. This delay caused anxiety to their companions who alerted rescue teams.

JULY 24—A girl became ill with an upset stomach whilst walking with friends on Ben Macdui.

JULY 27—A climber twisted his knee in the Lairig Ghru.

AUGUST 4—A family of three were reported to be in a distressed condition at the Pools of Dee, Lairig Ghru. An eight-hour search failed to trace them. It later transpired that the family were never in difficulties. The person who reported the incident had wrongly assessed the condition of the party.

AUGUST 10—A father and youth of 16, with no experience, no map or compass, and wearing shoes, set off from Etchachan Bothy for Jean's Hut via Ben Macdui. They became separated in perfect visibility and weather and were finally reunited at the Cairngorm Car Park.

SEPTEMBER 3—A walker en route—Crathie, Lochnagar, Glenmuick Car Park became overdue.

OCTOBER 9—Shortly before dark a young woman on holiday in the Knockando area set off to climb Roys Hill, a short distance from the house. She turned up 18 miles away in Dunphail the following day unharmed.

OCTOBER 22—A party of two walked from Cairngorm to the slabs of Garbh Uisge Beag, intending to go up Ben Macdui and then camp at Loch Avon. They left their rucksacks at the slabs and set off for Macdui. The weather deteriorated and so one of the pair returned to his rucksack and camped. He did not see his companion again and reported him overdue. Meanwhile, his companion had been found and looked after overnight by a party in the Shelter Stone.

NOVEMBER 30—A climber unroped on ice in Winter Corrie, Clova, fell about 15 feet. He was found unconscious.

DECEMBER 28—After completing a climb in Coire-an-t-Sneachda two climbers decided to walk back to the Car Park instead of waiting for the rest of the party who had the map and compass. In fact they walked down Coire Raibeirt past the Fords of Avon Bothy and a long way down the Waters of Caiplich. When they realised the seriousness of the situation they returned to the Bothy, arriving there the next day they were picked up shortly afterwards.

DECEMBER 28—A climber was injured by an avalanche in Coire an Lochain. Weather at the time was severe.

SOUTHERN HIGHLANDS

JANUARY 17—Two well-equipped and experienced hillwalkers were benighted on Beinn Dothaidh. They were picked up unharmed next morning.

FEBRUARY 13—Two hill walkers were descending An Caisteal without crampons in whiteout conditions. One slipped, lost his ice axe and disappeared. After a night search he was found the next morning. He is thought to have fallen about 300 feet and sustained a dislocated elbow, twisted knee and exposure.

FEBRUARY 13—Three experienced mountaineers were climbing *Central Gully*, Beinn Dothaidh in bad weather. Whilst the leader was negotiating the cornice part of it collapsed and all three fell for about 150 feet on steep snow when their rope snagged on a rock. All were uninjured. They dug a snowhole and waited for rescue the following morning.

MARCH 10—Two youths with exposure were rescued on Creag Tharsuinn.

APRIL 3—A female hillwalker, one of a party of four, was descending a snow slope on Stob Binnien. While glissading she lost her footing then her ice axe and slid out of control between 500 and 700 feet, sustaining a Wedge fracture of the 5th vertebrae, 5-inch laceration of the scalp and bruising.

APRIL 7—A hillwalker was injured on Beinn Glas.

APRIL 10—An experienced hillwalker was descending the gully separating Beinn Oss and Beinn Dubhchraig with two companions, when he disappeared from sight. His companions found him 100 feet further down the hill unconscious and badly injured. He died a week later without regaining consciousness. The cause appeared to be a simple slip on loose scree and ice.

MAY 8—Two adults and a 12-year-old boy, with no ice axes and wearing shoes became stuck on hard snow on Ben Lomond and had to be assisted to safety.

JUNE 1—Diabetic Dutchman overdue on Ben Lomond. Located near foot of hill unharmed 01.00 hours 2nd June.

JUNE 4—One of a party of poorly-equipped youths on a charity climb on Drumgoyne, Campsie Fells, was hit on the head and knocked unconscious by a stone dislodged by another member of the party.

JUNE 30—A young Swedish girl was evacuated from half way up the Ben Lomond path with a suspected broken ankle. She was wearing wellington boots and slipped on a rough part of the track.

JULY 2—Youth suffered exposure whilst on leadership exercise on the Ochil Hills.

JULY 31—A search was initiated for a man reported to have collapsed on Ben Lomond. Despite a fairly long night search he was not located. It later transpired that he made his own way down and did not inform anyone.

AUGUST 2—A 12-year-old Boy Scout under an experienced leader became unwell, apparently suffering from exposure due to heavy rain and strong wind, on Meall Reamhar, Killin.

AUGUST 5—An 18-year-old American girl, poorly equipped and in casual shoes, went for an evening walk on Stob an Fhithich, Ardlui. Whilst walking on steep ground she lost her footing and fell about 40 feet before stopping among some large boulders, she then attempted to crawl to safety and fell a further 15 feet, sustaining severe bruising of the back. It is unlikely that this would have happened had she been wearing proper footwear.

AUGUST 14—A 52-year-old man was reported to have had a heart attack near the summit of Ben Lomond. Examination revealed he was suffering from exhaustion and he was evacuated by stretcher. The incident was caused by the man trying to keep up with the younger members of the party.

GLENCOE

FEBRUARY 12—Whilst glissading down the west face of An t-Sròn, a hillwalker lost control and fell about 2,000 feet, suffering fatal head injuries.

FEBRUARY 20—Two climbers benighted on Buachaille Etive Mór.

MARCH 21—Two injured climbers. A party under instruction, having completed a snow and ice climb, were descending the West Face of Beinn Fhada, into the Coire bed by glissading. They climbed down the upper steep slope to the lower gentle slope and after the instructor and one other person had glissaded safely to the foot, the two injured took a slightly different route, lost control and suffered injury.

MARCH 26—A party of two and an instructor left to climb to Ossians Cave, but after reaching it decided to continue on to the summit of Aonach Dubh. They were caught in a shower of snow and decided to snowhole for the night, suffering slight exposure. Their equipment was adequate for the original climb but not for being benighted.

APRIL 8—A climber slipped and fell from the North West Gully of Stob Coire nam Beith, a distance of approx 1,500 feet and received fatal head injuries.

MAY—Man had heart attack on Ben Starav—helicopter rescue.

MAY 30—Experienced and well equipped walker tripped descending path at side of Clachaig Gully. Fell 300 feet. Fatal head injuries.

JULY 31—Walker removed from Fionn Ghleann—exposure.

NOVEMBER 8—Dutch marine had slight fall in Lagangarbh Coire. Found to be suffering from severe exposure.

AUGUST 21—A hillwalker slipped on a boulder field whilst descending from the Aonach Eagach ridge and broke his leg.

SEPTEMBER 17—A hillwalker had a fatal fall between Stob Coire nan Lochan and Bidean Nam Bian.

SEPTEMBER 17—A climber fell on North Face Route, Central Buttress, Buachaille Etive Mór and suffered back and leg injuries.

NOVEMBER 12—A climber on Curved Ridge (unroped) slipped on wet snow and fell 50 feet into Easy Gully, breaking her ankle.

NOVEMBER 27—Five university students benighted on Sròn na Creise. One girl slight exposure. Poor judgment and little help from rest of club.

DECEMBER 11—Two crag fast walkers were evacuated from Stob Coire nam Beith.

DECEMBER 17—Woman slipped and dislocated shoulder on Stob Coire nam Beith. Walked part way down, then stretchered.

DECEMBER 31—An injured climber was evacuated from the top of Lost Valley, Glencoe.

CREAG MEAGHAIDH

JANUARY 29—A well-equipped and experienced mountaineer was climbing unroped just below the summit. His crampons tangled with his clothing and he fell backwards about 500 feet down the slope, finishing up in a small snow cave, sustaining severe bruising and lacerations.

JULY 12—A hillwalker was evacuated from Creag Meaghaidh suffering from exposure.

DECEMBER 11—A party of two (father and 10-year-old son) got lost in a whiteout on Creag Meaghaidh. After spending the night in a snowhole, they were rescued unharmed the following morning.

BEN NEVIS, MAMORES and ARDGOUR

JANUARY 5—Injured hillwalker. A hillwalker glissading down the west face of Càrn Mór Dearg, without using an ice axe, fell awkwardly and dislocated his shoulder.

JANUARY 21—A party of poorly-equipped tourists ascended Ben Nevis. Near the summit one collapsed. Help was summoned but when the helicopter arrived there was no casualty. Apparently after collapsing from exhaustion and being unconscious for a short time he decided to walk down when he came round. Later located by helicopter. Dressed in shorts, thin shirt and lightweight cagoule.

FEBRUARY 3—Avalanched climbers. Two experienced climbers were climbing the final pitch of South Castle Gully. The leader was climbing round the cornice with his second belayed 30 feet below, when the cornice broke away carrying both 800 feet down the mountain. The leader was buried and his second, with a severely injured right arm, tried to dig him out, without success. Rescue Teams found him dead under 6 feet of snow. Avalanche warnings were displayed and the whole mountain was avalanche prone.

FEBRUARY 12—Injured hillwalker. A girl descending Beinn a' Chlachair, on hard snow slipped, tried to stop using her ice axe, hit a patch of rock and lost control. She finished up in soft snow with the ice axe embedded in her leg.

FEBRUARY 15—Fatal climbing accident. Two climbers were climbing in the area of Garadh Gully when the deceased, owing to exhaustion decided to return to the C.I.C. hut. His companion completed the climb, returned to the C.I.C. hut and found no trace of him. A search was made of the Garadh Gully and eventually the deceased was found buried 6 feet deep in avalanche debris. The weather was bad and avalanche conditions prevailing.

FEBRUARY 21—Fatal climbing accident. The deceased was with another boy and a teacher climbing Castle Ridge in good conditions. They had completed the greater part of the ridge and the teacher and the deceased were on a large stance and the second boy was climbing up to them, but having a little difficulty. The deceased it is believed, had taken off his crampons, went over to the edge to shout down instructions to the second boy, when he suddenly slipped and fell. He was later found dead with a fractured skull.

MARCH 24—Missing hillwalker. A couple descending Ben Nevis became separated. The girl was found dead in the vicinity of Five Finger Gully.

MARCH 29—Two injured climbers. Three climbers took a wrong bearing after climbing 3 or 4 Gully. On the descent they were caught in a small avalanche in Coire Eoghainn.

APRIL 2—A climber with a fractured pelvis was taken off Ben Nevis.

APRIL 17—An injured climber was evacuated from Tower Ridge.

APRIL 20—Fallen climber. A climber was killed when a cornice collapsed on Point Five Gully, Ben Nevis.

JUNE 4—A tourist fell while crossing the Waterslide in Glen Nevis and sustained fatal injuries.

JULY 2—A German tourist slipped whilst descending Redburn Gully, breaking a leg and wrist.

JULY 4—A German tourist was left behind by his three companions on the Tourist Path above the Youth Hostel. He eventually arrived at the campsite after taking the wrong direction in Glen Nevis.

AUGUST 9—A tourist was taken off the Tourist Path on Ben Nevis with a broken leg.

AUGUST 21—A female Pakistani tourist, who suffered from acute asthma, took 8 hours to reach the summit of Ben Nevis. She collapsed on the way down. She was wearing town clothes and open-toed sandals.

OCTOBER 15—A female hillwalker was descending the Tourist Path on Ben Nevis with three friends when she became separated. She was last seen in the zig-zags below Red Burn Gully and eventually found just below the C.I.C. Hut. She had no map or compass.

OCTOBER 15—Injured tourist. Returning from the summit of Ben Nevis a tourist slipped and sprained her ankle.

ISLE OF SKYE

APRIL 7—Fallen climber. The party had ascended Sgùrr Nan Gillean via the tourist route. They were descending via an abseil. The casualty got to the bottom of the rope then slipped, possibly on fresh snow covering hard snow ice, sustaining multiple injuries. The victim was from a large inexperienced party without ice axes or crampons.

APRIL 9—A climber fell on Sgùrr nan Gillean. Rescue services were alerted but he walked off uninjured.

APRIL 16—Injured hillwalker. Casualty and three others ascended Sgùrr Alasdair from Coir a' Ghrunnda (south facing and clear of snow) when they came to descend they did not like returning via their ascent and tried the Great Stone Shoot (North facing) which was full of hard snow and ice. No ice axes, crampons or rope in party. Casualty fell about 75 feet landing on a patch of scree, sustaining head injuries and broken humerus.

MAY 30—Injured climber evacuated from Sgùrr Sgumain.

MAY 30—A well-equipped climber fell on the Alasdair Stone Shoot and broke a leg.

JULY 10—A hillwalker collapsed and died of a heart attack in the Quiraing.

JULY 28/29—A man, wife and dog went to Coruisk from Kilmarie via Camasunary to the Bad Step. They did not like it and so returned to Camasunary, went up Glen Sligachan to join the Coruisk path at 6 p.m. They did not like the Bad Step from this side either and started to return to Camasunary via the Sligachan route. The wife twisted her knee and they were benighted. They eventually arrived back in Kilmarie at 8.30 a.m.

JULY 26—A climber tripped and broke an ankle on the Alasdair Stone Shoot.

AUGUST 6—Injured climber. The casualty and three others were climbing Sanguinary Cracks when he slipped on loose rock sustaining back and arm injuries.

SEPTEMBER 16—Fallen climber. The casualty was an 18-year-old boy climbing with a friend of the same age, on the West Ridge of Sgùrr nan Gillean, at the Gendarme. They were on their first visit to Skye and their first day out. They had seconded V.S. on outcrops but never been on mountains. They did not have a rope. The casualty was seen to go round the *Gendarme* on the Lota Coire side. He fell about 200 feet and was killed.

NORTHERN HIGHLANDS

JANUARY 8—A 16-year-old boy with a party of experienced mountaineers, was traversing the pinnacles on Spidean a' Choire Leith, Torridon, when he lost his balance on loose rock, slid for about 200 feet then went over the edge of a gully and fell another 30 feet on to snow. He sustained a fractured elbow, jaw, lacerations and exposure.

JULY 21—A hillwalker was evacuated with head, leg and back injuries after a fall on Beinn Bhan, Applecross.

AUGUST 4—Female walker evacuated from Creagan Meall Horn with suspected appendicitis.

NOVEMBER 3—A couple reported three days overdue in the vicinity of Dunbeg Bothy were located unharmed. The rescue incident was caused through a misunderstanding.

ARRAN

APRIL 8—On Friday, 8th April, at 10.00 a 57-year-old female hillwalker set off with two companions to walk to the A'Chir Ridge. On the way up she complained of pains in her chest but her companions were not unduly worried. By early afternoon, after reaching the summit of Beinn A' Chliabhain conditions had worsened. It was snowing, very misty and there were patches of soft snow on ice. Because they had no ice axes the party decided to turn back just below the A' Chir Ridge. On the descent the woman slipped on snow and ice and slid for about 15 feet, sustaining bruising to her right thigh. At 15.45 she felt sick and dizzy and a short time later fainted. Arran M.R.T. evacuated the woman that evening and she was found to be suffering from bruising, shock and possibly hypothermia.

APRIL 12—At 10.50 hours on Tuesday, 12th April, two male hillwalkers, aged 42 and 35, set off from Glen Rosa to traverse A'Chir Ridge, A'Chir, Cir Mhór, Loch na Davie, Glen Easan Biorach to Lochranza. At 15.00 hours in deteriorating weather they became separated. The leader was unable to locate the second man and descended for help. Shortly after the search began information was received that the missing man had made his way to Lochranza and booked into the Youth Hostel.

MAY 7—At 10.45 on Saturday, 7th May, 1977, a party of eleven Scouts and four Supervisors set off from Corrie to walk up Goatfell. Weather conditions were very wet, high wind and poor visibility. After the group had walked some distance two of the boys were very tired. The leader then decided to send four boys back with a Supervisor. On the way down they stopped for something to eat. It was then that the 10-year-old boy was found to be suffering from hypothermia and unable to move. Help was summoned and the boy evacuated by stretcher.

AUGUST 5—A well-equipped and experienced family of three were descending from Loch na Davie when their son put his foot in a hole and twisted his knee.

SOUTHERN UPLANDS

JUNE 12—A 56-year-old man hill walking on Rig of Craig Gilbert, with his son dislodged a rock which rolled on to his ankle and trapped him.

JULY 2—An American climbing in a quarry near Edinburgh fell and broke a leg.

JULY 5—An American tourist fell off Arthur's Seat, Edinburgh, and sustained head cuts and a dislocated shoulder.

We have omitted a number of incidents which are not directly connected with mountaineering or hill walking. These include several involving skiers (two fatalities), and false alarms involving mysterious lights seen on the hill. However:

JANUARY 11—A helicopter with pilot and cameraman was filming in the Loch Avon area when it developed mechanical trouble and made a forced landing on the frozen loch. The crew attempted to walk back to Glenmore via Strathnethy. They fired off red flares and were located and rescued by helicopter. The cameraman had slight exposure and bruising.

—It may well be safer on foot, after all.

And as an illustration of the hazards of matrimony. . . . JULY 10—A climber got her wedding ring stuck in a crack whilst climbing Savage Slit on Coire an Lochain.

REGIONAL DISTRIBUTION

As in previous years we have compiled this table from the preceding list of accidents.

	Casualties (of which fatalities bracketed)				Incidents No. of Direct Rescues	Call-Outs				Total Incidents
	Injury	Exposure	Illness	Total	Casualties	Cragfast, etc.	Lost	Overdue or Benighted	False Alarms	
Cairngorms Deeside	13	1	2(1)	16(1)	16	–	4	5	4	29
Southern Highlands	7(1)	4	1	12(1)	11	1	–	3	1	16
Glencoe	11(4)	2	1	14(4)	13	1	–	3	1	18
Creag Meaghaidh	1	1	–	2	2	–	–	1	–	3
Ben Nevis Mamores Ardgour	16(6)	–	1	17(6)	14	–	1	1	1	17
Skye	7(1)	–	1(1)	8(2)	8	–	–	1	1	10
Northern Highlands	2	–	1	3	3	–	–	–	1	4
Arran	2	1	–	3	3	–	–	–	1	4
Southern Uplands	3	–	–	3	3	–	–	–	–	3
All Areas	62(12)	9	7(2)	78(14)	73	2	5	14	10	104

IN MEMORIAM

C. E. ANDREAE

C. E. (EDDY) ANDREAE, a member of the Club since 1925, died on 21st November of last year. His fully active days as a climber covered the years 1922 until 1926, in which latter year he received an appointment as a civil engineer in the Public Works Department of the (then) Crown Colony of Nigeria. Becoming engaged in 1944 he was joined by his fiancee and married in Lagos in February 1945. There followed in 1952 an appointment with the Air Ministry in London, which Ministry was later merged into the Ministry of Public Works. His Nigerian and London appointments—he was a Londoner—put paid to all but occasional visits to the hills thereafter but those years 1922-26 were very productive. They are recorded by him in fascinating detail in the *Journal* under the title 'Early Days' (*S.M.C.J.*, 1975, xxx, 312), for he was one of those greatly responsible for the inauguration of the J.M.C.S. and, indeed, became its first President. Many of the most vivid recollections of those early days are of the training weekends on the Cobbler when (though other members of the party may have availed themselves of alternate transport) Eddy unfailingly cycled to Arrochar and back, after the Sunday's climb. The same locomotion took him further afield to the Crianlarich mountains. He was a prodigious cyclist and, indeed, in the summer of 1923 he cycled to London, spending four vigorous days with A. J. Frazer and myself on the Lakeland hills before completing his journey to London. The fact that I met him by appointment at Lesmahagow and, having 4½ horsepower available, towed him to Seathwaite, does not detract from this feat. At that time, before the S.M.C. Guides were published, we relied greatly on G. & D. Abraham's 'British Mountain Climbs' in which the Lakeland climbs were described in minute detail.

The most outstanding features of those years, though, were the five nights in the old half-way hut on Ben Nevis in March 1924 with Rutherford and myself, when we were described in the local press as 'Three Knights of the Alpenstock'—the hut survived only one more winter. He spent a fortnight in the summer of the same year with Hutchison, Rutherford and myself in Skye. We camped in Glen Brittle and by Loch Brittle and accomplished a satisfactory number of climbs in the Cuillin before a sprained ankle on Eddy's part, our disintegrating boots, and problems of transport brought an energetic and enjoyable, and in some ways a pioneering holiday (for the Skye Guide had only just been published) to an end. I cannot omit mentioning that Eddy's cycle bore him to Skye and back and perhaps it is not surprising that, on the journey north, due to engine trouble on the part of those relying on motorised transport, he reached Fort William some hours ahead of the rest of the party.

Although recently in indifferent health, his death came as a great shock to his many friends. We extend our deepest sympathy to his widow.

K.K.H.

BEN HUMBLE

B. H. HUMBLE, M.B.E., died in Aviemore of a stroke, aged 73, while working on a farewell speech to the Mountain Rescue Committee of Scotland. Formerly of Dumbarton and Arrochar, he was one of a family of eight brothers, of whom two are still alive.

Ben was a pioneer in dental radiology, but was forced to give up practising as a dentist due to deafness in 1935. However, this handicap did not inhibit his enjoyment of the Scottish mountain scene to which he increasingly turned, nor did it prevent him making a marked impact on that scene, right to the end of his life.

Douglas Scott was a companion of his early years in the hills and writes:—

'Ben was such a bundle of energy, such a vital person, that it is been a sore burden, but the effect only made him work harder. He difficult to realise that he is dead. The handicap of his deafness must have seemed to have an uncanny knack of knowing what had just been said, when, for example, at an A.G.M. he would get to his feet and floor his opponent without having read the notes passed to him.

'I first met Ben in Skye about fifty years ago. It had been a blazing hot day and his face was shining to match the setting sun. He had just come down from the Storr ridge after doing all the tops and his glowing account filled me with envy. At that time neither of us knew any climbers, so we naturally joined forces, sharing our inexperience. Looking through our old diaries now it seems a wonder that we had no serious mishap. Having no other contacts possibly made us more than usually cautious.

'His enormous capacity for research soon led to the treasure house of the *Journals*. In 1931 he joined the J.M.C.S., laid aside his shepherd's crook and we bought ice axes. He was interested almost from the start in the reasons for mountain accidents, and rescue organisation. On his first visit to the Cairngorms he recorded seeing the cairn by the Shelter Stone "where Ellis the English student died of exhaustion."

'Arrochar was his early spiritual home. Indeed it was difficult in those days to get much further in a short weekend by the old Link Line bus, or on bicycles. He always kept a diary of his excursions, and when we shared them, gave me a copy. They have all the freshness of real adventure and a feeling for a good story. His writing was prolific, articles and letters innumerable, to friends, and others, to the Press. Also books, illustrated by his own photographs, for he was an enthusiast with a camera. And, although on occasions he might answer, "Oh, they didn't come out." There were many more when his results were superb, with fine composition and atmosphere.

'Here is a glimpse of Ben from his diary of a vintage weekend on the Arrochar hills: "8th June 1930. Terribly cold, but visibility at 4 a.m. was glorious. The best view we have ever had from the Cobbler. Shortly after we were startled to see mist coming down over Ben Ime. That was only the beginning, . . . everything blotted out . . . colder and colder. We missed the map now but thought we could get to Ben Ime without it . . . soon hopelessly lost. Walked about for two hours in dense mist. At last we got clear, 9 a.m. now and eight miles from Arrochar. Passed through the village at 11.30, hadn't even the energy to make a cup of tea . . . slept for two hours and felt better. Our intention . . . to get the bus at Inverbeg . . . started to run and were within twenty-five yds. of the road at 7.15 when the last bus passed. Just had to hoof it another six miles to Luss."

'A man of gusto, that was Ben.'

He was, as everyone must know, stone deaf, and that may well have been the root of his remarkableness, an absolute commitment to involvement and thus communication. He became well known as an author and photographer, contributing articles to magazines such as *The Scots Magazine* and *Climber and Rambler* and writing a number of books which included *On Scottish Hills*, *Tramping in Skye*, *The Songs of Skye*, *Wayfaring Around Scotland* and *The Cuillin of Skye*. The last was a painstakingly researched and well illustrated mountaineering history of the Cuillin, now long out of print and much in demand by collectors. Skye was one of his greatest loves and in 1930 he helped to organise the first Skye Week which is now a well established event in the island's calendar.

It is appropriate that Ben's best known and probably his own favourite photograph is of the Cioch silhouetted against a sunset cloud sea, 'a picture of a lifetime' as he himself described it.

He was also an early movie maker in mountains and made a film of an ascent of the South Peak of the Cobbler which is still good to see. It incorporates something of Ben's risqué humour in its scene of two lady climbers discarding their skirts behind a rock.

Ben's canvas of mountain interests was wide and his energy and involvement did not diminish with advancing years. He was the only Club member for whom the President and *Journal* Editor were well advised to maintain an individual correspondence file. His letters came on all subjects—Dinners, A.G.M's, Huts, Publications, politics, etiquette, and of course, accidents and rescue. Ben was into everything, right up to the end of his life. It was uncannily fitting that a letter from him appeared in *The Scotsman* on the day of his funeral. As somebody said 'Ben always had the last word!'

Perhaps the most remarkable thing about all this was that his opinion was always worth listening to and frequently later proved to be accurate. Eric Langmuir makes this tribute—'I often took his advice on matters concerning Mountain Rescue. On those few occasions when I acted against his advice, I was always proved wrong. When you really get down to it, Ben's life was one of unstinting service. The material rewards he obtained for his work were trifling compared to what he contributed.'

He was probably best known for his contribution to Mountain Rescue and his concern about accidents. This extended over some 40 years or more and merited the award of an M.B.E. He used the first mountain rescue stretcher in Scotland and was influential in the founding of an independent Mountain Rescue Committee for Scotland, his views ensuring that this work became the responsibility of the rescue teams rather than the climbing clubs, as in England. He was a member of the Committee from its inception and his consistent effort was to ensure the independence of the Committee and the Teams from control by those, such as the Police, with a statutory responsibility for rescue. In this his work is of lasting importance as he has helped to ensure that the control of mountain rescue work remains in the hands of those who actually do the job.

Due to Ben's work as Recorder for the M.R.C.S., there exists today a complete record of incidents over more than 20 years. This is invaluable for any kind of investigation into accident and rescue trends. Anyone involved in M.R. work will appreciate the difficulties he had, to extract reports and information from the Teams, most of which have a healthy unconcern with reporting and filing. It was a daunting task which he tackled with characteristic vigour and determination.

As a close friend of Donald Duff, the pioneer of the Duff stretcher and another stalwart of the Scottish Rescue scene, he was the moving force behind the highly successful Duff Memorial Exhibition *Adventure in Safety*, which opened in Glasgow in 1968 and was subsequently held in London (1969), Edinburgh (1970) Aberdeen and Fort William (1972).

The Duff Exhibition gave large numbers of young people the opportunity to see at first hand the need for skill and care in their hill walking. This was especially important to Ben who had a profound concern and enthusiasm for ensuring that young people were introduced to the hills in the best possible way. He was associated with Glenmore Lodge since the early days when it was housed in what is now Loch Morlich Youth Hostel. He acted as a voluntary instructor for over 15 years and when he became less able to lead the way on the hills he turned his boundless energy towards the creation of an alpine garden in front of the Lodge. He cared for it steadfastly over the years and it remains a memorial to him and to the things he cared for.

Ben had a happy gift of establishing a rapport with those of a later generation than his own. Des Rubens says—'I regretted the death of Ben Humble very much. Several of the E.U.M.C. came to know him quite well in the last few years. I think it is worth noting that we were very impressed by his enthusiasm for his own latest excursions, both abroad and at home, and his interest in the activities of young climbers like ourselves. We in turn were fascinated by that remarkable scrap book, his other personal records and not least by the eccentric manner of the man himself. It is our regret that these visits of ours to Feithlinn were to come to an end so soon.'

Ben valued his continuing links with Glenmore Lodge in the later part of his life. He was there a good deal, his arrival heralded by those great sighing 'Aaaahs' which one heard first as he came through the front door. His departure announced by the fierce, clutch-destroying revving of his car, by which he projected himself up the front drive and away home to Aviemore. He was a guest at a number of Hogmanay dinners where his recital of the 'Ryvoan Rat Farm' astounded and amused successive students.

He was a grand man and we miss him. One cannot but speculate what Ben might say if he could reach across the gulf and comment on what we have written about him. It might well be—'Not bad, not bad, but if you had asked me to do it in the first place I could have done it better myself . . . . Aaaaaah!'

F.W.J.H.
E.D.G.L.
W.D.B.

JAMES EARL MacEWEN

To HIS many friends he was always—EARL—and so he will remain. He and I were guests at the 1941 New Year Meet at Crianlarich and, together with J. H. B. Bell, enjoyed a great day over the ridges of Bidean in splendid conditions of hard snow and brilliant sun. He joined the Club the same year, and with very few exceptions attended every winter Meet until 1968 when, increasingly, arthritis was to curtail his activities. He served on the Committee during 1946/49, and looked after *Journal* advertising in the same period.

Born in Stirling in 1906, he was educated at the High School there and in the north of England, and thereafter joined the family firm of D. & J. MacEwen & Co. He soon took on responsibility for running their subsidiary the MacEwen (Stirling) Grain Co., and in that capacity had the opportunity of meeting a great number of the farming community up and down the country. This association doubtless sharpened Earl's interest in weather and the seasons, an interest which dovetailed nicely into his other passions of climbing, ski-ing and angling.

During the War he served as a Captain in the 7th Battalion, Argyll and Sutherland Highlanders, being through the Dunkirk evacuation, and returning to Europe shortly after D-day.

Although Earl had skied pre-war, it was possibly the snowy winter of 1947 that convinced him of the possibilities of this form of transport. That winter many farms were cut off from the outside world by impassable snowdrifts. With others, Earl concerned himself with taking in supplies to some of them and he so enjoyed the use of skis at this time that henceforth their use became a part of his mountain life. By 1953 skis and mountains had become combined as his ideal. The Haute Route, at that time unpopularised, gave him a glimpse of the big mountains in their pristine state—Breithorn, Pigne d'Arolla, Mont Blanc de Seilon, Ruinette and others. Before this year he had climbed amongst the summer Alps, mostly in the Valais where his best climbs were the Matterhorn, Weisshorn, and the Wellenkuppe—Ober Gabelhorn—Arbengrat traverse.

Back home, ski-touring became his major mountain interest. As Convenor of the S.S.C. Stirling Section, and a major instigator of the Stirling Ski Club, he was a tremendous source of knowledge and encouragement to the local youth. For more than twenty years he made the S.S.C. hut on Ben Ghlas his special care. That it has survived so many winters is itself a tribute to his devotion.

One of the first references to Earl in the *Journal* is of himself and Bell on the Slav route to take pictures of the Orion face. He was an accomplished photographer, as illustrations in the *Journal*, and that of the S.S.C. bear testimony. Older members will recall with pleasure some of his slide shows at N.Y. Meets.

Primarily Earl was a man of the hills, his long legs carrying him easily over miles of high ground, and he loved every aspect of the mountains. But above all he was an all-round country lover and will be greatly missed by his many friends with like interests.

J.D.B.W.

EDWARD CHRISTIE THOMSON

THROUGH the death in June 1977 of Edward Christie Thomson the Club has lost one of its senior members, a former Past President, and a man who was devoted not only to the Club but to the Scottish mountains.

Thomson had a great capacity for friendship. He had a fine character and was himself the most loyal and reliable friend. In his last years he was less active but the warmth of his welcome at Club functions was in itself a real tribute to the great regard felt for him by members.

Born in Edinburgh in 1897 he was educated at Merchiston Castle School and in 1915 went from there direct to the Army where he served in France as an officer in a heavy artillery unit. After the war he qualified as a Chartered Accountant.

I knew him first when he joined (ex President) Harry MacRobert's office in Glasgow to which he came for wider industrial experience. Later we moved separately to another office where there were two Club members: Norman Mowbray and W. B. Speirs. Together we climbed for some years until he moved back to Edinburgh. I followed east too at that time in 1934 and we were close friends for over 40 years.

As a Club member Thomson served as Custodian 1925, Committee member 1928-29, Hon. Treasurer 1925-36 and as Vice-President 1945-47 and President 1954-56. To all these posts he brought great purpose. In 1937 his work was referred to by J. H. B. Bell in a note in the April *Journal*.

A cultured and imaginative man, his interests were wide. Based on a simple and deeply held faith he was an elder in the Church of Scotland. His hobbies were astronomy, meteorology and in particular a passion for music to which he devoted much time—he accompanied the Club song at dinners for many years. But in great part his first love was climbing. His knowledge of topography was immense as was his knowledge of the Club.

He became a member in 1920, knew and climbed with several original members and their successors and recalled with great affection their kindness to him. It is interesting to note how this remained with him. In April, 1950, he wrote a *Journal* article called 'The S.M.C. Genealogical Tree' in which he traced the descent of every member then from the original founders. His own ancestry led from W. A. Smith (O.M.), William Douglas, Harold Raeburn and Charles Inglis Clark—a goodly succession of forebears.

At his first Club Meet in 1921 at Killin, he had the pleasure of a lesson in rock climbing from Harold Raeburn, and his first climb was up Beinn Laoigh by the main couloir; on this occasion one of his company was Stanley Harrison, our present Hon. President.

He participated on the Cobbler at the 'cave' meet in August, 1925, when he and I joined the meet as late arrivals to meet Rusk Hutchison and Rutherford. At this Meet, as all know, the J.M.C.S. came into being. His own interest was the subsequent development of the Club by thorough training of younger men, of whom I was one. I think this interest stemmed in part from some days in March, 1925, when with others he spent days looking on Benn Achaladair for a climbing casualty (*S.M.C.J.*, 1925, xvii).

Thomson was not one of the modern school of mountaineers, but climbed all his life. He maintained a detailed diary from boyhood days of every ascent he made—with names of his party and other notes—not only in Scotland but in Austria, Switzerland, the Dolomites and in Ireland. Most of these days would bring back special memories on re-reading.

He covered Scotland, from Cheviot to Ben Hope, much of it by cycle. He made many of the traditional winter and summer ascents, Nevis, Glencoe and Skye being his special areas. I think Blaven may have been his favourite hill, and it is good to know that in 1971 he climbed it again with his wife—I think it was his last Munro.

He liked occasions, and with Harry MacRobert and myself went up Nevis by the Lower Ridge to hansel the unveiling of the S.M.C. Indicator in 1927. Always reliable as leader and companion I remember his bringing us back to Glenmore Lodge from the slopes of Ben Macdhui roped up in the teeth of a north-east hurricane which hid our feet until he walked over a cornice on Cairn Lochan.

But these personal reminiscences and records in his life do no more than exemplify his deep love for the Club and the hills. To these can be added by others who knew him their own permanent experiences with him and who can record themselves the loss we have now sustained.

He had a very happy married life, and to his devoted wife and his daughter and sons we now offer our sincere sympathy.

R. R. ELTON.

IAN REILLY

IAN REILLY was killed in January, 1978, along with his companion, Brian Simpson, whilst climbing on Creag Meaghaidh.

Ian's talents ran to more than mere climbing competence. His climbing career developed along with that of his twin brother, Gerarde, and together they shared equal enthusiasm and climbed many fine routes. As well as being skilled on both rock and ice, his quiet enthusiasm and sharp sense of humour always seemed to inspire others, no matter what the situation. In addition Ian had done a considerable amount of climbing instruction, both for the local Education Authority in Dundee and for the Youth Hostel Association in Glen Brittle.

An extremely popular character on the Scottish climbing scene, Ian will be sadly missed by all friends and relations.

G.M.

As we go to print we hear with regret of the death of Frederick Mantz in a climbing accident in Glencoe.

PROCEEDINGS OF THE CLUB

Easter Meet 1977—Braemar

THE Easter Meet held at Braemar Lodge Hotel was attended by 19 members and 5 guests.

The weather was very good throughout and ascents were made every day and from reports received included: Glas Maol, Cairn of Claise, Càrn an Tuirc, Creag Leacach, Càrn Aighe, Glas Tulaichean, An Socach, Beinn Iutharn Bheag and Mhór, Mam nan Càrn, Lochnagar, Càrn a'Choire, Beinn Bhreac, Beinn a' Chaorruinn, An Diollard, Càrn an t-Sagairt Mór, Cairn Bannoch, Fafernie, Càrn Aosda, Càrn a' Gheóidh and the Cairnwell.

The ski mountaineers traversed Càrn an Tuirc, Tolmount and Tom Buidhe, Cairn of Claise and Garbh Choire and from the Cairnwell to Càrn a' Gheóidh.

Present were: President Donaldson, D. J. Bennet, M. H. Cooke, R. R. Elton, R. G. Folkard, C. C. Gorrie, J. N. Ledingham, R. C. S. Low, W. M. MacKenzie, K. Macrae, J. R. Marshall, H. H. Mills, M. Morrison, T. Nicholson, G. S. Roger, B. G. S. Ward, C. B. M. Warren, W. T. Taylor and F. R. Wylie, and guests: J. Bell, J. Broadfoot, C. Elton, J. Nicholson and O. Turnbull.

It was a most enjoyable meet and we express our thanks to Mr McKay and his staff at Braemar Lodge Hotel for looking after us so well and to the President and his wife for their kind hospitality.

New Year Meet 1978—Glenspean

THE New Year Meet was based at Glenspean Lodge Hotel with a few staying nearby.

The weather was somewhat unsettled but quite a few ascents were reported including: Beinn na Lap, Beinn a' Chlachair, Creag Pitridh, Geal Chàrn, Stob Ban, Stob Choire Claurigh and Geal Chàrn (by Dalwhinnie) and some members penetrated the recesses of Glen Pean, the Leanachan Forest and snow filled Glen Roy.

Present were 15 members and 1 guest: President Donaldson, D. J. Bennet, A. G. Cousins, C. C. Gorrie, J. N. Ledingham, I. D. McNicol, D. H. McPherson, H. H. Mills, T. Nicholson, G. S. Roger, D. Scott, I. H. M. Smart, A. Sommerville, C. B. M. Warren, F. R. Wylie, and J. Broadfoot (guest).

Despite the weather a good time was had by all and we would like to express our thanks to Mr and Mrs Smith and their staff at Glen Spean Lodge Hotel for looking after us so well and to Douglas Scott and his wife for their very kind hospitality.

Reception, A.G.M. and Dinner, 1977

S.M.C. DINNER time again, and a Saturday dawned unusually dark, wet and misty even for the abysmally bad autumn and early winter of 1977. We would not be missing a marvellous day's weather for the hill. The Club met for the second time at Stirling, and the very good turn-out for the dinner as well as the other events showed that this had been a popular choice. Shoppers jammed the pavements. Then through the Golden Lion's doors came a different world by sudden contrast, thick carpets, Victorian pillars, people you hadn't seen for a year, much talk of that wonderful Sunday two weekends before when all Scotland basked in frosty sun, windless air, and bright colour.

Summoned to the palatial lecture room, we met Mr Don Aldridge, who lectured on 'The Adventures of Limpet Smith.' A change from the usual climbing lecture, it gave a half hour trip into unreality. Each slide was a coloured cartoon drawn by the author, illustrating various fallacies that the general public believe about mountaineering and that mountaineers believe about mountaineering. The scores of slides must have involved an immense amount of artistic work, and the lecturer used projectors in unison, tape-recorded music and his own spontaneous comments to heighten the unreality. At one point, the hotel receptionist caused the biggest laugh of the lecture by coming on the air with loud incomprehensible remarks just at a critical moment when the lecturer stood poised dramatically over his equipment with the audience wondering what would happen next. This reviewer is ashamed to admit that the air of unreality became so well maintained that he fell asleep for a second, waking up with a sudden jerk of the head and then furtively looking round to see if his neighbours had noticed, but all seemed under the spell of Mr Svengali. Finally the lights went up, we saw Don Aldridge, and we thanked him for the immense skill and work that he had put in and for coming to give us what was a unique lecture.

There followed tea. A solitary waitress stood behind a long table groaning under sandwiches, cups, tea, and biscuits. No particular end of the table indicated start or finish. The result, with a couple of hundred members and guests, was a cross between a scrum and an anarchic free-for-all. Anyone polite by nature was left tea-less. Darwin's 'survival of the fittest' operated, and interestingly the fittest turned out to be not necessarily the youngest and strongest, but the oldest and wiliest. A few venerable members were to be seen standing confidently behind the table along with the distracted waitress, grabbing sandwiches and pouring cups of tea. It was an interesting practical illustration of the well-known scientific law that the more people are present and the more individualistic they are (i.e. S.M.C. members and such-like), the index of disorganisation and inefficiency increases as the square of the number present and the cube of their individual cussedness.

So much so that by the time some had just drunk their tea, the summons had already come for the A.G.M. This proceeded at smooth and remarkable speed, apart from several unexpected but interesting interludes. In the first, Sandy Cousins wished an offending word in the previous A.G.M. minutes deleted, and after a brief verbal skirmish with the secretary got his way with what seemed full Club backing, although many members looked puzzled about what it was all about. Next, Kenneth M. Andrew asked for action over the threat of nuclear waste being dumped in Galloway, and possibly other Scottish hills (Outer Hebrides, Western Highlands, Cuillin, Cairngorms). This surprise produced a long, disconcerted silence from the office-bearers. Such occasions at the S.M.C. are marked by the secretary, ostrich-like, scrawling notes feverishly, and the chair blinking distractedly while wondering what on earth to say. Rescue came with a proposal from the floor for Mr Andrew to be our nuclear watchdog, so that the Club could object immediately an application to dump waste went to the district council. Dougie Niven of the Club's main watchdog group then asked us to object to the proposed pumped storage scheme at Craig Royston on the east side of Loch Lomond, just north of Ben Lomond, and Tom Weir ably backed him with a rousing speech packed with information. We agreed with Tom's proposal to press for the existing scheme at Loch Sloy to be used for pumped storage, and to call for a planning commission instead of the usual public inquiry, so that the debate could be opened more widely to include alternatives like Loch Sloy, and not just restricted to the one issue of Craig Royston. All were agreed until somebody ended this particular discussion by saying in a few years we'd have self-government anyway, whereupon the A.G.M's loudest cheers burst forth. Unfortunately, no one could use them to decide on a bet on the result of the forthcoming referendum, as it proved impossible to determine whether the shouts of even one's neighbours were jubilantly backing the speaker's remark or were vehemently objecting to it. Amidst this pleasant confusion we congratulated George Peat on being elected an honorary member for his long services to the Club, and proceeded to rubber-stamp all the Committee's decisions about office-bearers and committee within a few swift seconds. Now, feet started to scratch the floor, heads to nod, and other such intention movements to begin in anticipation of the sudden rush to the bar. Ah, but there was still any other competent business! Trevor Ransley could hardly have chosen a worse time to praise the importance of females to the social side of mountaineering! Amid a stream of hisses, he immediately went on the defensive, hastily explaining that he meant just asking them to the S.M.C. dinner and not—horror of horrors—suggesting they might be considered for Club membership. Tom Weir brought the meeting rapidly nearer its end by boldly interjecting 'I oppose that totally!' Our wily secretary then discovered that Trevor Ransley's proposal was inadmissible, as the five weeks' due notice had not been given, whereupon Trevor ended by saying he was now giving one year's notice that it should be discussed at the next A.G.M.!

Pleasant imbibings followed at the bar, and later we were ushered into a bigger and more palatial room for the dinner. The tables had been arranged around the walls, leaving a vast space in the middle as if a dinner dance was scheduled, not a mountaineering dinner. Was it a plot by Trevor Ransley? At any Club dinner, this writer fills up like a car on fuel, and afterwards can never remember what the food or drink was, far less what it tasted like, so this gets the problem of writing about it neatly out of the way! The atmosphere at least was good enough for the chorus of the Club song to be rendered with much more vigour than usual, despite the errors printed on the dinner card. Spirits rose so high that shouts of encore rang out. Jim Donaldson, complete in kilt and dancing shoes, called out that the night was young and advanced nimbly into the vast space in the middle of the room calling 'What about an eightsome?' but alas, the replete slothful company ignored this too masochistic presidential appeal to our nationalistic sal-vationism. During the interval, Iain Macleod played the bagpipes to great effect in a nearby room. After apologising for being a poor substitute for the Club's resident psychopath, who was absent in America, Rob Richardson nevertheless soon launched into veiled insults and comments deflating to the Club's guests. J. Butters of the Scottish Ski Club replied with a mixture of praise of the S.M.C. quotations about ski-ing from the early Club *Journals* and hints about the guilt feelings of S.M.C. members about their ski-ing activities on the piste. Jim Donaldson then brought the formal proceedings to a pleasant end, having guided his first meeting as S.M.C. President with dignity and benign good humour. Later, many were unwilling to go, enjoying the lively atmosphere and good company to the last. Finally out into the streets and a different reality, enjoying the sight of the grand old buildings on the way to car parks, sharing the night air with the high spirits of Stirling folk just out of the pubs, and then out into the damp black night and a foretaste of the next day's bad weather for the hill. The S.M.C. dinner over again and yes, it was a good one.

A. WATSON.

J.M.C.S. REPORTS

We lead off with welcoming back to the Club the re-born J.M.C.S. Section at Inverness; we are more than a little envious of their strategic situation and wish them all success in this favoured territory.

Inverness Section.—The Section, despite a slow beginning, has thrived since its revival last Easter with a membership of some 27 active climbers. Although the Section holds monthly hut meets, members are encouraged to climb and explore the North West as an informal group rather than as a large organised party—one active pair have already enjoyed winter routes on Cul Mór, Cul Beag and Beinn Dearg. Other members have been active on Nevis, Lochnagar, etc., and a notable first ascent was made by the Section President and an S.M.C. companion in Glen Strathfarrar.

During the coming year two members are participating in an expedition to Baffin Island with another pair, visiting the Gavarnie Cirque in the Pyrenees in April. Several more will be making the annual pilgrimage to the Alps and one explorer is off to Iceland.

Nearer home, meets are planned to Carnmore, Foinaven and other points north while the Section's first Annual Dinner will be held later this year.

Office bearers—President, Gerry Smith; *Vice-President*, Steve Carroll; *Secretary/Treasurer*, Mike Phimister, Alt Dearg, 4 Old Mill Lane, Inverness.

Edinburgh Section.—All in all a satisfactory year with all the meets well attended by both younger and older members of the Section. Hopefully the senior members will continue to get out regularly as this is going to be beneficial to our up and coming new recruits, both young and old.

Most of our new members need more experience and training in winter climbing conditions and techniques. Unfortunately this has been hindered over the last months by very bad conditions out on the hill. Nevertheless I'm sure their enthusiasm will carry over to next season.

Sadly an era has come to an end. This section of the Club has been all male throughout its history. However, we have been under pressure for some time now from a large number of our members to admit women to the Club as full members and this is now the case.

Hon. President, Mike Fleming; *Hon. Vice-President*, Jim Clark; *Hon. Member*, Ian M. Ogilvie, O.B.E.; *President*, F. Fotheringham; *Vice-President*, D. Mor; *Treasurer*, Bill Myles; *Hut Custodian (the Smiddy)*, Jim Clark; *Committee Members*, A. Dunn, A. Morris, N. Grant, I. Brodie, K. McCulloch; *Secretary*, Pete Myles, 59 Morningside Park, Edinburgh, EH10 5EZ.

Glasgow Section.—Again the Club has been very active in all areas, with many of the harder classics receiving ascents by a small core of activists.

Winter and autumn meets were particularly well attended. We were very fortunate with two of the best weekends of the winter being spent on Ben Nevis.

Summer meets were poorly attended and once or twice had to be cancelled. However, one healthy trend which developed was the breakdown of established climbing partnerships and the evolution of an extremely active group of about ten members who teamed up not only at weekends but during the week for frequent flying visits to Glencoe. Even Creag an Dubh Loch received (successfully) a day visit.

Dumbarton Rock has now become established as a Club training ground (for falling off as well as climbing). Also it acts as a focal point during the spring and summer where the weekend's schemes are hatched.

Socially the Club has had a very successful year. The Annual Dinner was held in the Kingshouse Hotel where we once again enjoyed the indulgent hospitality of Jim Lees and his staff. Retiring President Pete Hodgkiss received a small token for the work he has done for the Club over the years. Hamish and Curly were their usual incorrigible selves and led the 'choir' virtually non-stop most of the night. The undoubted highlight of the weekend was the completion of his final Munro by Jim Donaldson. No mean feat after the dinner. Our congratulations to him.

The Burns' Supper was once again held in the Brabloch Hotel, Paisley, where we were entertained by excellent speeches from Alex Small, Bill Young, Mary MacKenzie and other weel kent faces. The previous years' high standard being maintained. A special thanks to those who attended despite the grade V roads outside.

The Friday lectures were well attended culminating in the photographic competition which was judged by Bill Young (to give the rest of us a chance of winning). His critical and witty commentary was appreciated by the large attendance.

The Coruisk Hut lease has been extended for a further 10 years and is well used by other clubs, providing a steady source of income under the hardworking custodianship of Murray Easton.

Membership stands at 80 with a number of keen and experienced prospective members about to join the Club.

Office bearers—Hon. President, Ian Burley; *Hon. Vice-President*, Gordon Ross; *President*, Alastair MacGregor; *Vice-President*, Hamish Henderson; *Treasurer*, Bill Forbes, 11 Hillside Road, Dundee; *Secretary*, Donald Stewart, 18 Buchanan Drive, Cambuslang, Glasgow.

Lochaber Section.—The membership has remained around the 75 mark now for the last few years. As the Club is located in one of the best climbing areas in Scotland access to the hills and the availability of climbing partners is not a problem for local climbers. Because of this there is not the same demand on the Club as compared to a 'city' club for organised meets and transport. It is, therefore, to the credit of the members that a successful climbing club does exist in Lochaber. Only six outdoor meets are held over the season. Four during the winter, usually in kindred huts and the yearly 'Lake District' and 'Island' meets. The Lake District meet is always very popular, probably due to the change in beer, despite the poor weather which besets us every year. The 1977 island meet was to Rhum in mid-May at the start of the dry and sunny period. This year's island meet is to Coruisk on Skye to which it is hoped to sail by chartered boat from Arisaig.

A keen and active committee has organised a successful season of slide shows and the Annual Dinner Dance over the winter period. Most of the speakers were local or friends of the Club and shows given were varied, very good and inexpensive. 1977 saw a record attendance at the Dinner Dance, and the Annual General Meeting. Two of our members also completed the Munro's. Under the enthusiastic and able hut custodian, extensive repairs have been carried out to Steall Cottage, the Club hut. Gas fires have been installed, the whole repainted, and a new toilet ceremoniously placed. Further work is planned to make Steall one of the better huts in Scotland.

The committee are now engaged on raising money for a Club meet to the Engadine Alps in 1979.

Office bearers—Hon. President, J. Ness; *President*, D. Watt; *Vice-President*, J. Patterson; *Treasurer*, W. Adam; *Hon. Secretary*, L. Houlker, No. 3 Treslaig, Ardgour, by Fort William; *Hut Custodian*, E. Kay, 22 Glenloy Street, Caol, Fort William.

Perth Section.—Membership of the Perth Section was, at 54, down by 5 on the previous year. Thirteen meets were held during the year of which three were day meets and ten weekend meets. Meets were well attended in the main and were normally blessed with good weather.

The highlight of the year was an exceptional long weekend on Skye during which time the Cuillin was blitzed by Section members, the only complaint being that there was no breeze to disperse the heat haze! On a cultural note we won the 'Mountain-Mind' trophy at a quiz organised by the Carn Dearg Club.

Our Section Dinner saw us in Glencoe. The undisputed excellence of the accommodation at Lagangarbh was matched by the hospitality of the Kingshouse Hotel where we dined.

The Joint Annual Lecture with the Perthshire Society of Natural Science was given by Myrtle Simpson. Her first-rate lecture gave us a look into one of the largely unvisited mountain regions of South America—the Cordillera Blanca in the Peruvian Andes.

The A.G.M. was held in Perth on 18th November. Following the usual reports and elections a variety of topics were discussed, the most important of which was the impending Jubilee of the Perth Section. Jubilee year is 1979/80 and will begin with a meet at Easter to Coylumbridge—the scene of the Section's first meet.

On a less happy note I have to report the death of our second Honorary Member within a year. James Miller had been a member of the Perth J.M.C.S. since 1946, although his first 'Munro' was bagged during the last century. Naturally, his active hill days had finished some years ago but there will be many members of longer standing in the Club who will remember and miss him.

Office bearers—Hon. President, Chris Rudie; Hon. Vice-President, John Proom; Hon. Members, David Wares and Walter Pethers; President, Ken Layhe; Vice-President, Iain Robertson; Treasurer, John Rogers; Secretary, John Reed, 9 Burnbank, Bridge of Earn, Perth.

50th JUBILEE YEAR—1979-80:—Any former Perth Section Members who are no longer on the mailing list but who are interested in attending the Jubilee celebrations should contact John Reed.

London Section.—It has been a good and active year for the Section as it continues to mature into an established club south of the Border. Many parties visited Scotland during the winter with further trips in the summer, indicating the renewed interest in Munros. Little was achieved in the Alps. However, Section members took part in four separate expeditions to the Himalayas.

Our three Welsh winter meets in January, February and at Easter all had some snow enabling many routes to be completed. In fact, by mid November the snow had returned in sufficient quantities to produce a few quality winter routes—a rare occurrence in north Wales. The main summer meets were centred on mountain crags, Cwm Silyn and Cwm Eigiau in Wales and at Ardgour in conjunction with the Glasgow Section.

Section finances are reported to be in an extremely healthy state, due mainly to the lack of major expenditure on Glenafon cottage to date. The sixty or so members seem to be an unusually dependable bunch with few outstanding monies. The intake of new members was again around the half dozen mark.

On the social scene, we again held our Section A.G.M. and Dinner at the Waterloo Motel in Betws y Coed and were entertained and enthralled by an excellent slide show given by Leni Smith on his Nanda Devi trip. We hosted the Whole Club A.G.M. and Dinner at the Wastdale Hotel in March, attended the Whole Club Meet(?) in June, the Glasgow Section Dinner, the B.M.C. A.G.M. in Wales, were represented by Hugh Jordan on the B.M.C. South East Committee and were allowed to patronise the Savoy Tavern for yet another year.

Office bearers—*Hon. President*, Joe Della Porta; *President and Treasurer*, Dave Edmunds, 70 Buryfield Road, Olton, Solihull, W. Midlands; *Secretary and B.M.C. Representative*, Hugh Jordan, Waytes Cottage, Layham Lane, Keston, Kent; *Glenafon Hut Booking Secretary*, Bill Wheeler, 142 Priory Lane, Roehampton, London, SW15.

S.M.C. AND J.M.C.S. ABROAD

The Alps

A. G. COUSINS, J. M. TAYLOR, D. R. GRIEVE, D. J. PYPER, W. D. BROOKER, with W. Morrison and Alan McNicol traversed the High Level Route on ski from Argentière to Zermatt during the last week of April, 1977.

They went by the Argentière and Trient Huts, with J.M.T., D.R.G., W.M. and A.M. diverging to include the Aiguille du Tour en route. Enormous quantities of snow obscured most crevasses and rendered it possible to enter the Val d'Arpette by the Trient ice fall and Col des Escandies, but an abominable breakable crust made the going difficult for the weaker skiers. At Bourg St. Pierre SLESSER appeared, full of new-found Italian enthusiasms and Eurocratic vigour. While A.G.C. and W.D.B. went to collect the transport the rest slogged their way up to the Valsorey hut, only to return next day in low cloud and a blinding storm of wet snow which effectively put the Plateau de Couloir route past the Grand Combin out of reach and sent a thwarted Slesser back to Italy. The alternative from Verbier was then adopted and from the Mont Fort hut a splendid day of perfect weather was enjoyed in traversing the Rosa Blanche to the Dix hut.

Dubious weather returned and the Pigne d'Arolla was traversed in cloud to reach the Vignettes hut, A.G.C., D.J.P. and W.D.B. going in more leisurely fashion by the Pas des Chèvres. The last and perhaps the finest stage of the H.L.R. was marred by deteriorating weather and poor visibility, Zermatt being reached in lowering cloud, snow and finally heavy rain. The snow continued to fall for the next 48 hours and plans to continue to Saas Fee were abandoned. Thus ended the Gerontocrats ski-outing, the party finally leaving Zermatt to the swarming Japanese without even having had a glimpse of the Matterhorn.

In spite of the varied weather, it was an interesting and enjoyable trip. Anyone wishing advice or information about this route will be able to choose from seven different versions on application to the various members.

J. McK. STEWART writes, 'In August I visited the Bernese West and Zermatt area with Geoff Pearson and his wife Marjorie.

'Starting from the old Sanetsch Inn above Zion, we climbed Les Diablerets by the Tsanfleuron Glacier and N.E. ridge. On the 7th, we did The Wildhorn by the Brotest Glacier, retreating just short of the summit and experiencing severe weather conditions on route back to Inn. Next day, descent to valley and up to Leukerbad before proceeding to the Lämmern Hut where on the 10th, we assisted in a helicopter search and rescue of climbers missing on the Schwarzhorn and so to the Schwarenbach Inn.

'On the 11th, in perfect conditions we climbed the Balmhorn by the Schwarz Glacier and Zackengrat and the following morning crossed over the Gemmipass and on to Zermatt before ascending to the Gandegg Hut. On Sunday 14th, a fine freezing morning, we went up the Theodul Glacier to the Breithorn by its S.W. face, two of the party went to the upper bergschrund at 4,000 m. line whilst Geoff continued to summit, with descent to Gandegg and on to Schwarzsee for the night.

'On the 15th, to Stafelalp and up to the Schönbiel Hut from where next day, Geoff and I set off for the Pte. de Zinal, weather deteriorated on the Höhwang Glacier, exploding over us on the Col Durand into a violent storm which drove us back to the Hut and down to Zermatt. 17th, up to the Täsch Hut, weather broken returned to Zermatt and spent the last few days in Zinal at Hut level only.'

LEN SMITH (J.M.C.S.) reports his 1976 activities as follows.—'From mid July to the end of August I completed 37 routes, 24 in ascent. I spent the first week warming up in Chamonix. Routes included Aiguille De L'M by the Couzy Route, T.D., in heavy rain; Aiguille Pelerins by the Crouton Ridge, T.D., from Montenvers and, best of all, the Petit Dru by the North Face, T.D.+. This last route was done with a Swedish climber named Olf. On the first day we reached the balcony above the Niche and sat the night out in heavy snow. Next day the route to just below the summit was badly verglassed and made progress so slow we bivouacked yet again, this time in a fierce thunder storm. Day three saw us up and over the summit followed by a rappel descent down the south west ridge.

'A few weeks later I was back in the same area, this time with IAN VAN HINSBERG (J.M.C.S.). The highlight of our stay was an exacting one-day traverse of the Auguille du Géant, Aiguille de Rochfort, Dome de Rochefort and Mont Mallet. I then teamed up with Jim Fairey and in the next nine days climbed the following routes: Pyramid du Tacul by the East Ridge, finishing at the Trident hut; Mont Maudit by the Frontier Ridge followed by a bivouac outside the Cosmique hut; Aiguille du Midi by the Frendo Spur in two days; the Cosmique Arête solo in 45 minutes to the Trident hut; Mont Blanc by the Route Major during which we were hit by constant stonefall and finally a traverse of Mont Blanc, Mont Maudit and Mont Blanc du Tacul and so down the Midi téléphérique.'

JOHN FAIRLEY (J.M.C.S.) and wife (resident in Germany) again had an active season, mainly ski-ing. This included a week's touring in the Otztal and an ascent of the Wildspitze. They also made ascents of the Bergseechijen by the South Ridge, the Schijenstock by the South Ridge and the Freiheit by the South Face.

Corsica

GEORGE ROGER writes: 'I was very fortunate in being asked to join DAN LIVINGSTONE, BARCLAY BRAITHWAITE and HAMISH HAMILTON for a holiday in Corsica in September. Dan very kindly took us in his caravette and moreover did all the driving in Corsica and all the cooking; he knew the island well from earlier visits. We landed at Calvi and drove over to the east and up the Golo valley to Albertacce. We went up Monte Cinto from the south, staying at the Erco hut (built in 1975) and had a most pleasant day in perfect weather and were accompanied by a very friendly dog. Thence we drove over Col de Vergio and two days later set off from the col up the Golo valley and bivouacked in one of the Tulla begeries whence we did Pagha Orba from the Col des Maures—another very enjoyable day despite mist and sleet on the summit. The view of Capo Tafonato with mist swirling round its rocky ridges and through the famous hole was very impressive. Later we went south and crossed the Col de Bavella, an excellent climbing centre. Unfortunately the weather was wet and misty so we returned northwards and visited the Restonica and Asco valleys en route for Cap Corse. From Olcani we walked up to the Bocca Di Giovanni. Dan and I went north to Monte Canelo while Hamish and Barclay went south to Monte Corvo. This was my first visit to Corsica—a most impressive island—and I look forward to the next visit.'

Spain

A. L. CRAM writes: 'My wife and I paid another visit to the Picos de Europa, in N. Spain, during late June to early August, expecting weather better than experienced last year in May and June. Once more a Land Rover was taken for use on the high mining roads for access to the high pastures. Camp pitched near Las Monetas, in the upper Rio Duje valley, was washed out the first night. Refuge was found in a Spanish household in the mountain village of Sotres. As it is important to know the way down in bad weather before venturing too high among the complexities of limestone walls and canyons, a number of days were spent on the lesser tops of the northern end of the Macizo Oriental, each requiring a long walk, the earth roads being too mired for wheels. Eventually, on a day of mixed weather we reached Ceuta Tejao 2128 m., Mazarassa 2158 m., Sorinan 2168 m. and the Pico de Valdominguera 2266 m. An effect of the white mist on the white limestone was to give an unusual brilliance to the alpine flowers, especially the gentians. This variety and quantity of alpines was quite exceptional in our experience of Iberian mountains.

'Red dashes on my map, drawn to show a route up the Canelón de Vierro and then up its true right cliffs to the Collado de Valdominguero with access to the central tops of the East Massif, lured us, with mist down to base, into the trackless complexities of the Canelón, not a scrap of which we had ever seen. Repelled at every attempt to force a way out by steep gravels or escarpments, we continued up the 1000 m. high arroyo, to a sharp crest with an impressive drop on the other side. On this col, the clouds suddenly were sucked down, revealing we were about a mile to the South West of the Collado with the central peaks in between and on the easy rocks leading up to the Pico de Cortes 2370 . Then all sank into the smother. Later, as we groped down the hindrances of the Canelón, I was relieved to see all trace of the escape route hidden in mist as I sensed an observation about route-finding, however in unknown arroyos, was struggling to escape from my wife. Luckily, she became happily diverted by recognizing a cairn she had built to mark the locality of the Land Rover which was indistinguishable among huge rocks, at the time. The day was however not over. The drive up the headwaters of the Duje to the Refugio de Aliva, is comparable to the track from Loch Pattack to Culra Lodge in Ben Alder Forest and a great deal worse than from Attadale House to Bendronaig Lodge. Even a faint cattle trail seemed a lure to better ground, but it turned along the mighty spur, known as La Lomba, towards the wall of the Macizo Central. Turning became impracticable on the steep-sided sharp crest and, eventually, I halted at a steep declivity in the crest. Casting forward on foot, a glance back showed the Land Rover, apparently high above my head on a suspension bridge in a tunnel of cloud. A cattle trail led round some rock spires down to the neck which was crossed by a mining road of sorts. My wife, meantime, mused by herself, in the car, sitting high up in the clouds, with now zero visibility and rain.

'One sunny day we traversed the rocks of the Pico Santa Ana 2602 m. down to the hard nevé of the Collado Santa Ana and then reversed back to make a second ascent of the Peña Vieja 2613 m. The weather broke again. From a camp on the Puerto San Glorio we had a long circuit in the Cordillera Cantabrica, over the rugged Zamburria 2107 m. and other tops of the Peña Prieta group to the east of the pass.

'From a camp on the Collado Panderruedas 1550 m. we made second ascents of the neighbouring tops, but an attempt to follow the old road to the Macizo Occidental over the Vieja and Dobres cols ended in exhaustion in soaking hangs of impenetrable scrub in the clouds. We were glad to see our tent once more. Driven by rain into a hospedaje in Posada de Valdéon, we set off in poor weather for the Torre Bermeja 2393 m., spending some four hours in steep wet scrub on the way to the Collado de Burro 2108 m. but seeing two of the rare rebeccos (rupicabra) at close quarters. We arrived back just before the deluge, which affected the roads, causing us to move to the south side of the Picos but it continued from time to time at camps on the Embalsa de Ruesga and the Embalsa de Ebro and later in a more spectacular manner in our flight eastwards through the drenched Ebro Valley.'

South America

RAYMOND SIMPSON writes: 'My wife Linda and I have just returned from seven months travelling in South America; we carried enough climbing gear to enable us to attempt a number of peaks in the Cordillera Blanca on our own, and in Ecuador I was fortunate enough to climb several peaks with members of the 'International Andean Mountaineers.' This is a Quinto based club of predominantly Scots climbers who are in the fortunate position of being able to climb Andean peaks on a weekend basis—all the year round.

'We started travelling at the end of June and our first objectives were the attractive peaks of the Cordillera Callaraju, at the southern extremity of the Cordillera Blanca; there we climbed Nevado Shamakrasu by its North ridge and Nevado Brazil, the highest of the group by its west face; there is no record of a previous ascent from this side. Both peaks are around 18,600 ft.

'We then moved farther North and climbed Nevado Jatun-monte-punchu from the Quilquayhuanca valley by its long and complex West ridge. In neither of these areas did we meet any other climbers or see any indication of climbing activity. This was not the case, however, when we moved up to the Parc National Huascaran where we met six expeditions and two large trekking/climbing parties from C.A.F. and Mountain Travel. In this area we climbed Pisco, an easy peak of 19,000+ ft., but an excellent view point. We also climbed the North face of Yanapatcha Ouest. This was a very fine climb which does not appear to have been done before.

'In September and October we crossed the Andes and descended to the jungle on two occasions, in Peru and Bolivia, by five- and six-day trails masterfully engineered during the Inca period.

'In Ecuador I climbed Cotopaxi, 19,400 and Chimborazo, 20,400 with Stuart Murray, and Tungerauha on my own. We also climbed Illiniza Sur and Altar with George Gibson; the latter gave us a memorable ascent over the Christmas period. We left our high camp at midnight on Christmas day and reached the summit at dawn after over 2,000 feet of fine ice climbing illuminated by a full moon and lava bombs from the nearby active volcano Sangay (17,000 ft.). Roast guinea pigs for Christmas dinner were only slightly less bizarre than an eightsome reel danced by kilted Scots in the back yard of George's jungle residence on Hogmanay. Objective danger was present in the form of a five-foot-deep stagnant sewage ditch. A hundred-mile canoe trip on the Rio Napo was our last adventure before returning to Scotland at the end of January.'

ROBERT J. WATTERS (J.M.C.S.) writes: '1977 was a quiet year. After climbing Mt. Citlaltepec in Mexico, we carried on by truck to Argentina. The major excitement en route was negotiating a cheap and safe method of transporting the vehicle between Panama and South America.

'While in Argentina I climbed Aconcagua, the highest peak in the Western hemisphere at around 23,000 feet, in February. Two Argentine climbers, Daniel Palacois and Mario Aguirre accompanied me to the summit, by the North route. My own colleague, Tom Molloy (Colorado Mountain Club) had succumbed to frostbite and altitude lower down on the mountain.

'The main problems on the mountain are not technical. Cold, snow storms and altitude are the difficulties to be overcome, and the summit day was reminiscent of a good winter's day on the Ben. The entire trip took some 18 days from Puente Del Inca via the Horcones Valley to the summit and back, including two days obtaining the necessary Police and Army permission. This permission is required as the peak is close by the Chile/Argentine border and also, as access to the mountain is relatively easy, ill-equipped and unfit parties are kept out of the area to reduce the accident rate. The two days spent obtaining permission entail equipment checks and running for 15 minutes at 9,000 feet to check blood pressure, etc. Hence once you survive these two days, the hill is easy in comparison.

'If any Club members head down that way look up Luis Alberto Parra, the Police official in Mendoza, who will provide much needed assistance.'

Asia

LEN SMITH (J.M.C.S.) went to the Elburz mountains in Iran during April 1977 with Roger Reid and Frank Eastwood for a pre-Himalayan acclimitization trip and to test lightweight U/2 tents. During their ten days they climbed Darmand II and reached 16,000 ft. on Demuran but had to retreat because their tents failed in the high winds. Len reports that in April the high mountains present hostile conditions for climbers whereas the lower peaks are practicable on skis

GEORGE ROGER writes: 'MIKE Low kindly asked me to join his party of four for a trek through the mountains of Nepal in November. He did all the organising of the trek through Mountain Travel. The other two were DOUGLAS SCOTT and Don Lockhart (A.C. and Eagle Ski Club). From Kathmandu we drove west along the Pokhara road (completed in 1973) for about 80 miles to Dumre. Here the whole party of 20 consisting of 4 Sherpas, 12 porters and ourselves, set off on 4th November following the Marsyandi River northwards to its source about 100 miles away. Two days later we had wonderful views of Manaslu, Peak 29, Himal Chuli and Annapurna II. We camped in delightful spots and passed through Lamjung, Tordu, Darapani, Chame and Pisang (12,300 ft.) below Annapurna II. Thence westwards through very fine wooded country with frequent magnificent views of the Annapurna, massif and often at dawn inspiring views eastwards to Manaslu and Himal Chuli.

'We had a good look at Manang (12,500 ft.) built on an arid hillside. Here we left the Marsyandi and went up steep slopes above the Khangsar River heading west for our objective—the remote Lake Tilicho which was new ground for our Sherpas. We camped at over 15,000 ft. on 14th November and set off hopefully next day for the lake. We toiled up to a top of 17,000 ft. and had a great view of the Grand Barrier, Tilicho Peak, Roc Noire and behind it Annapurna I, but there was still another distant moraine to be surmounted to reach the lake which meant another camp further to the west. On the 17th we reached the top of this moraine and looked down on Lake Tilicho (16,140 ft.) below Tilicho Peak—a very rewarding view after much effort at that altitude. We returned to camp in great fettle and celebrated with a good dram of Glenfiddich followed by an excellent dinner. We returned eastwards next day crossing over the hills and camped above the Marsyandi beside a yak herdsman's tent. At dusk the whole herd of some 70 beasts were silhouetted against the evening sky coming down the ridge to the pastures beside us. Thence we had a steep descent and crossed the Marsyandi and followed it northwards camping on a grassy spot where we were joined by a large European party led by Norman Dyrenfurth going south. We were off at 6.20 next morning for the Thorong La and saw the source of the Marsyandi coming down from the glacier above through very impressive gorges. Thence up to the pass (17,770 ft.) and on to a small top to look down on a small frozen lochan. We left the top of the pass about 2.30 and descended by a steep path some 5,000 ft., latterly by moonlight and camped at the sacred village of Muktinath (12,500 ft.) at 7.30—a great day which called for appropriate celebration that night. Next morning at dawn we had a wonderful view of Dhaulagiri.

'We walked down the Jhong Khola to join the Kali Gandaki valley—an old trade route from Pokhara to Mustang still much in use. This is desert country and at mid-day a strong southerly wind blows up the valley. With heads down we walked over the stony flats by the river to Jomsom (9,000 ft.) where we spent the night and saw Dhaulagiri by moonlight. We continued south through arid country to Marpha where there were fields of crops and orchards of apples, oranges and bananas. Thence to Tukchek and down through fine wooded country with the roar of waterfalls from the river below passing through narrow gorges. We camped at Dana and as we watched the last rays of the setting sun lighting up Annapurna South and Fang the moon rose above the col—a most impressive sight. We continued by the Kali Gandaki to Tatopani where we crossed the river and went up the Ghar Khola to Ghorapani. We met many trains of donkeys and ponies carrying salt from Mustang to Pokhara. From Poon Hill (10,000 ft.) we had great views of Dhaulagiri and towards the Sanctuary with Annapurna South and Annapurna I and Machapuchere. Thence over the hills through very pleasant wooded country to our last camp at Hyanga. Next day, 29th November, we walked down the road to Pokhara and flew back to Kathmandu. So ended a most interesting and enjoyable trek right round the Annapurna massif. We covered over 200 miles in the course of 24 days.

'We record our thanks to Mountain Travel for their most efficient organisation. The Sherpas led by Passang Tsering were first class, and the porters worked very well indeed. The tents and sleeping bags were most comfortable and the meals cooked by Dorje were varied and most excellent.'

Himalayas

LEN SMITH (J.M.C.S.) was in a nine-man expedition to Nanda Devi in the 1977 pre-monsoon season. He reports as follows: 'Like all adventures ours was well spiced with unexpected trials. The Grenadier Guards who brought out our gear arrived late. Bad weather further delayed the long walk in and after two strikes and thirteen days of toil in foul conditions we reached base camp. In fact only two Lata porters reached this far, Kmal Das and Bal Singh, while the three high altitude porters, Kubrham, Bokurham and Chapperham bore the weight of low altitude load ferrying thus forfeiting their chances of going high on the mountain.

'These delays effectively wrecked our planned medical project and lost us the possibility of trying any new routes. Instead we concentrated on ascending the South Ridge of Nanda Devi. Four camps were established above base and two members reached the summit on 22nd June, followed by two others the next day. The success of the lead climbers was due largely to the effective support from below, from the two Manali men who stocked base camp and camp one and two of the soldiers, Nick and Tim, as well as the other members of the expedition, Arnold Pines, Roger Reid, John Miller and Frank Eastwood. It was they who undertook most of the unrewarding and boring task of ferrying loads up the mountain so that each camp was properly stocked.

'Conditions on the ascent were reasonably good, in fact the only bad snow was below camp one. The weather changed daily but held for most of the climb, although the early arrival of the monsoon hampered our descent and the evacuation of an injured climber took a week. Overall the route was nowhere above Alpine grade III, was surprisingly enjoyable and should be well within the capabilities of any experienced alpinist.

'The non-climbing Indian member, Lavkumar Kacher, made a preliminary conservation survey of the Nanda Devi sanctuary. He identified the major causes most likely to destroy the unique beauty of this area. These are the poaching of the Blue Himalayan Sheep, deforestation and the over grazing of domestic sheep during the summer. Added to this is the growing pressure of increased traffic into the Sanctuary through the gradual improvement of access paths. Subsequent recommendations have been made to give the area National Park status, thus controlling the activities of visiting expeditions and local herdsmen so that future conservation is assured.'

ALASTAIR MACGREGOR (J.M.C.S.) spent three weeks as a medical officer with a trekking group going into the Annapurna Sanctuary. The group set off from Pokhara and made their way along the Naudanda Ridge to descend into the Modi Khola at Chandrakot and from there followed the left bank into the Sanctuary. Unfortunately the lingering monsoon took its toll in way of an excess of leeches and only fleeting glimpses of the Annapurna Himal. However, once the Sanctuary was gained magnificent views of the Annapurnas and Machapuchere were enjoyed, similarly on the descent. With one other party member he had a day ascending the N.W. side of Hiunchilito a height of 15,000 ft. before turning back due to serac danger. Two cases of altitude sickness occurred—one being in one of the Sherpas! On the descent half the village of Chumro were entertained by his ineptitude at pulling out the teeth of the other half.

ANDREW RUSSELL (J.M.C.S., London Section) was on a two-man expedition to Nepal during the pre-monsoon season last year. The objective of the lightweight party was Sisne Himal, an unclimbed 21,000 ft. peak in the Kanjiroba district of north west Nepal. This region is very isolated and difficult of access, much of it uncharted.

From the airstrip at Jumla they trekked northwards and managed to set up base camp within a week. However, a reconnaisance made from an 18,000 ft. subsidiary peak showed that a northerly approach to the mountain was not feasible. Eventually, they decided to tackle the peak from the Jagdula basin which lay to the south. The route into the basin had only been accomplished once before over a difficult col. For over a week during April they threaded their way through the seracs and soft snow, stockpiling gear as they progressed.

Tragically, both climbers were swept by avalanche on 1st May and Andrew was suffocated. Richard Anderson, his companion, tried in vain to revive him but eventually had to give up, just managing to retreat to safety at base camp having escaped with a twisted leg and mild frostbite.

Andrew was totally committed to the big mountains of the world and his enthusiasm and knowledge will be sadly missed by the Section for many years to come.

DONALD MILL writes: 'HAMISH BROWN and I with five others—IAN VAN HINSBERGH, CHARLES KNOWLES, FRANK SCHWEITZER, STEPHEN SIMPSON and PETER STOKES (J.M.C.S.) visited the Nanda Devi basin in September/October 1977.

'We flew to Delhi, where we found a sufficiently wide range of food—apart from tinned meats—was available in India: Delhi for Western items, Rishi Kesh or Joshimath for staple foods such as rice, flour and ghee. We quickly learned to make chapattis which are excellent on their own or spread with jam, syrup, honey or whatever.

'A preliminary visit to the Bhyundar Valley, though too late for the best of the flowers, helped us to get fit and accustomed to camping at 14,000 feet.

'The party left Lata on 10th September, walking through the Rishi gorge during the tail-end of the monsoon, to arrive in the sanctuary on 18th September. From then until our departure we enjoyed unbelievably settled weather.

'Base camp at 14,000 feet by the Uttari Rishi glacier was a delightful spot with abundant wood and water and an ever-changing view of the snow peaks on the east rim. From here we made forays in twos and threes as we felt inclined. Because we had no mountaineering permit our activities were confined to 'trekking.' However, it is amazing how much a mere trekker can get around in the Sanctuary. Had we not all been gentlemen we might have been tempted to bag some of the smaller peaks and (since there was no liaison officer) no one would have been any the wiser.

'Rishi Kot, P6187, P6053 and Sakram, for example, looked to be elegant peaks easily climbed Alpine-style by a lightly equipped party, but the peak which impressed us most when we first saw it was P6401, at that time believed to be still virgin. A line from the Changabang glacier seemed to provide the easiest route to its summit, mostly on snow but with a 500-foot rock step which would have demanded strenuous climbing (too difficult for most members of our party) on what looked like excellent granite. The west side of this peak would give high-standard climbing on snow/ice. But of course these were mere pipe dreams. Our examination of these peaks had to be made through binoculars, from the safety of the level glaciers. Nevertheless, time passed all too quickly and everyone was reluctant to tear himself away when the porters arrived to help us out.

'The return journey through that tremendous gorge in absolutely still, clear air, was in some ways the most memorable part of the trip.

'It is worth noting that with careful planning a visit to the Sanctuary could comfortably be made from Scotland inside a three-week holiday. Best times for this would be early June or early October. At the time of writing no permit of any sort (not even a visa) is necessary for a walking trip, and the cost might be a pleasant surprise.'

Other Expeditions

The Edinburgh Kishtwar Expedition 1977.—We have received the following account from Des Rubens: 'The Edinburgh Kishtwar Expedition was a small budget, low key affair. It consisted of Rob Collister, Geoff Cohen and myself.

'On the first part of the trip, Geoff and I flew to Delhi at the beginning of July. We then enjoyed a ten-day warm-up in the beautiful Wadvan Valley of Kashmir. We were self-sufficient during this time, covering about a hundred and ten miles, crossing two high passes and climbing a peak of about 18,500 feet.

'The scenery in the lower reaches of these valleys was reminiscent of the surroundings of the easier Alpine peaks. Higher up, above permanent habitations, our way passed through magnificent gorge scenery which then gave way to alluvial plains with the main Himalaya beyond. The people we met varied from scores of villagers, accompanied by pack animals (including the odd dzo), on the first pass, to Bakerwali herdsmen passing the summer on the high pastures below the glacier snouts. Chapattis and delicious goatsmilk were often forthcoming from these friendly people.

'The main part of our expedition (despite its title) was spent in the Zanskar Tehsil of Ladakh. Rob joined us in Srinigar. A few days later, we started our walk up the Suru Valley, through Balti villages with barley fields nestling under the towering pyramid of Nun Kun. Near Ringdom Gompa, we came across our first Tibetan Buddhists. The total change of religion, race, dress and house style made us feel as if we had entered another land. Two days later, we shouldered 80 lb. packs, left the Pensi La, which divides Zanskar from the Suru Valley, and set off up the Durung Drum Glacier, a wide easy highway leading up to the heart of the mountains.

'In the ensuing two weeks, we climbed two fine mountains. Viewpoint Peak (c. 18,500 ft.) gave us a good climb and an opportunity to clarify our knowledge of the geography of the area. From the summit, we plotted a route up what was to become Delusion Peak (c. 20,000 ft.), a mountain on the Kashmir side of the watershed. This ascent involved us in several days of struggle. Our first attempt ended in defeat when we ran out of food after two snow-bound days on a ledge at 18,000 feet. The return to our food dump involved descending a rock rib and re-crossing a col to the Durung Drum Glacier. On our second, successful attempt, we climbed a continuously interesting route of about 4,000 (vertical) feet over a period of three days. Both bivouacs were unpleasant as the weather was generally bad. On the second morning, we obtained magnificent views of Nun Kun, Sickle Moon, the Brammah Peaks and a host of other Kishtwar and Zanskar Mountains.

'In retrospect, we enjoyed the challenge of climbing as a small party among these little-known peaks. It was agreeable to be so flexible and mobile, particularly in regard to the organisation of transport.

'Because of the continuing unsettled nature of the weather, we abandoned any further climbing and returned to the Pensi La. Our walk out through Zanskar was, in many ways, the most interesting part of the expedition. Zanskar is probably the most remote and least hospitable region of Ladakh, accessible only by high passes. The people are only beginning to be subject to modern influences (e.g. matches have still to come in in a big way!). We found the Buddhists hospitable, good humoured and religious.

'In three days, we reached Padam, where we split up. Geoff ploughed a solitary course over the Umasi La to the incredible gorge of the Chenab beyond Atholi and reached Kishtwar in five days. Meanwhile, Rob and I walked through deep arid gorges where the few villages hugged tiny spaces amongst a patchwork of ripening barley. Monasteries were built high above the river on impregnable defensive positions. At length, the gorges gave way to alluvial plains and these in turn to the high pastures and then glaciers of the Shingo La. The prayer flags at the summit marked the boundary between Ladakh and India. Next day, we crossed the final obstacle, a frightening melt water stream and descended to the first Lahoul villages, and then to Darcha.'

Greenland: The Harald Drever Memorial Project 1977.—The following are abstracts from the report on the above project by Dr P. W. F. Gribbon:

'For more than thirty years the late Professor Harald Drever, Department of Geology, University of St. Andrews, who was also one of our members, was intimately concerned with the people of the village of Igdlorssuit near Umanak in West Greenland.

'He made a lasting contribution to the preservation of one of their cultural skills when he initiated a kayak endurance race across 50 miles of open sea from Umanak to Igdlorssuit. He wished to ensure that both the art of kayak construction and its skilful use in the seal hunting was not lost to the Greenlanders who still followed a hunter's existence in a harsh, dangerous, yet beautiful environment. He had provided the prize monies; he had donated a handsome trophy for the winner. With his death, this race was in doubt. However, last year the future of the race was certain. The Umanak Kommune formed a committee to run the race. They started to raise support for future races. The kayak race is here to stay. The Harald Drever Memorial Fund to help the race funds was started last winter. A sum of about £1,700 was raised from over one hundred contributors scattered throughout the world. This sum has been matched by contributions from the Umanak Kommune and the Greenex Mining Company, which operates at Mamoralik in the Umanak district.

'We organised the Harald Drever Memorial Project as an expedition whose purpose was to go to Igdlorssuit. We wished to participate in its summer activities, to give the hut that Drever had used as a permanent base for his geological work to the village hunters federation and to see that his two boats in future would be used to the maximum benefit of the village. We also planned to re-ascend the highest mountain on Upernivik Island and rename it with his Greenlandic name, Aaralik. The University of St. Andrews party consisted of P. W. F. Gribbon, David Meldrum (who spoke Greenlandic), Adam Arnott, John Thurman, Colin Matheson and P. Gribbon.

'One morning in the bright sunlight the villagers assembled on the grass in front of the school. One of the village council, Hans Zeebl climbed on to a makeshift platform erected against the school wall and made a short speech in the Greenlandic tongue recalling how, for many years, Harald Drever had visited them to work and to be their friend. He pulled back a cloth covering the maroon letters emblazoned on a white background. It read: 'Aaraliup Atuarfia'—Harald's School, in translation. The villagers sang a short song and the simple ceremony was over.

'The Kayak Race was held on Saturday, 6th August. The course was over 16 miles from Umanak to Sermiarssuit on the Nugssuaq peninsula and back. Unfortunately only I, Dave and, by a card-drawing lottery, Adam, were able to cram into Hans Zeeb's speed-boat and to join the armada of small craft that accompanied the competitors across the calm sea. There were eleven participants drawn from Umanak and the surrounding settlements of Qaersut, Saatut, Nugatsiaq, and, of course, Igdlorssuit, while one kayaker came from Egedesminde, two days' sailing away from Umanak. We had our hopes on Kristian Nielsen from Igdlorssuit who had been the runner-up in 1976. While the kayaks waited on the starting line, a melee of power boats manouvred for position around the aquamarine speedboat, sporting the Danish flag, and waiting for Josef Motlzfeldt, the head teacher of the district, to discharge his upraised shotgun. Bang! The kayakers dipped their paddles, the boats surged forward. We patrolled the left flank. The kayaks spread out, with two kayakers in the van dipping paddle stroke to paddle stroke; one was Kristian Nielson, the other Georg Mathiessen, the winner in 1976, heading for the mainland. They rounded the marker boat, neck and neck, 8 miles to go. The convoy swept past icebergs outlined against the sun's reflections on the water. Umanak mountain loomed larger. The battle was on! There was no-one left to challenge them. Nielsen drew ahead, but Mathiessen gained the lead in his last effort. It was too much to sustain so that Nielsen again went in front with 400 yards to go. He paddled confidently into the harbour to disappear diffidently into the crowds. Every competitor received a well-deserved welcome; a bottle of squash was nectar. The prizes were awarded at a reception held in the Umanak community hall: no-one missed out. It had been an exciting afternoon . . . .

'Our party spent 10 days camped in the heart of Upernivik Island. Three tiny tents were perched on a moraine crest overlooking the broad snow fields to the jagged rocky peaks. They were the familiar mountains, the Horns of Upernivik, Merendi, Whaleback, Spume, Scorpio and others climbed by earlier St. Andrews expeditions. This was the dazzling glacier bowl first traversed by Drever in 1938. Slightly withdrawn, a slender pale rock spire above winding ridges dominated the northern sector. This was our objective: the summit of a 'great white tower.' At 2105 metres it was the highest point on the island. It had first been climbed by two members of Drever's 1950 expedition, Meldrum had been at its top in 1967, I had been there in 1969. It was our first choice, our raison d'etre . . . . We set out on a perfect morning in soft low light moving over the hard snow towards a sparkling col below the long south ridge. There were difficult pinnacles astride the ridge that we climbed directly on good rock, and some horrific snow slopes of loose glassy ice marbles that we turned with our legs like jelly with our crampons biting uncertainly into the steep slopes. Alternative rock staircases took us to a small niche under the summit block. We climbed singly up its last 30 ft. to a narrow rock springboard balanced over space; it had taken 11 hours of interesting and difficult climbing to reach the summit of Aaraliup qaqqaa—Harald's mountain. I stood on the top to say a few well-chosen appropriate words. We had a strong sense of ultimate fulfilment . . . .

'We returned to the glacier of Sermikavsak. We seem to have adopted it for St. Andrews as our own personal glacier. In the past we had surveyed and mapped its snout, we had kept tags on its recession, we had trailed selected boulders moving down its surface, we had noted the plant recolonisation on its foreland plain, we had related the lichen growth to its retreat rate, we had measured the electrical conductivities of its snow and ice. This time we were working on its surface features. Thurman drilled its surface, set up markers to measure its daily ablations, probed its dirt cones with thermometers, littered its surface with test patches of stones, gravel or sand, and kept cold 24-hour vigils. Thurman, Briggs and Arnott wandered with poles and measuring tapes to map the rise and fall and spread of a medial moraine emerging from an ice fall. Meldrum skirted the snout, surprised to find vegetation lurking in a gravel push-moraine perched on its face—Sermikavsak was again on the move towards the sea! The Gribbons wandered and wondered, and with measuring calipers they attacked the honeycombs of cryoconites burrowing into the ice. We were absorbed . . . .

'We climbed other hills in other places, we journeyed by the boat to other islands and highlands. We wandered in the rubble heaps of the Akuliaruseq hills. We waded the rivers swollen with snow melt water at Nerderlit, we endured the voracious mosquitoes of Karrats Island, we caught too many cod at Ubekendt and too few salmon at Itsako, we played football against the men of Nugatsiaq village, we returned always to our friends at Igdlorssuit . . . .

'We had achieved what we set out to do, and more, and I feel that Harald Drever would have approved of it all.'

REVIEWS

The Scottish Highlands.—By W. H. Murray. (1976; The Scottish Mountaineering Trust, 301 pp., 39 photographs and 18 maps. £6·50).

We have all become used to the S.M.C. District Guides and Climbers' Guides. Perhaps we even take them too much for granted. We all grew up with them. The new editions with their up-to-date information keep appearing, packed with detail invaluable to anybody seriously wishing to explore the Scottish hills, and yet invariably so handsome and well written that many who never go near a hill want to read them and buy them. Like the S.M.C. itself, they have a special character, up-to-date, international and modern in some ways, but in other ways timeless, individualistic and uniquely Scottish. When a rumour started a few years ago that the S.M.C. contemplated a new idea—a lavish book on the Scottish hills as a whole—more than a few heads were worried. The new book has now arrived. Clearly, no one need have worried about quality being sacrificed, with W. H. Murray taking on the job as author. Bill Murray has put his own individualistic stamp on what he was asked to do. He has produced a super-guide, something that looks like an S.M.C. District Guide and maintains or enlarges the best District Guide tradition, but in fact covers the whole of the Scottish Highlands in a masterly way. I have no hesitation in recommending it as the best guide so far published on the hill country of the Scottish Highlands.

The author says in his Introduction that the book is background reading by which the S.M.C. District Guides and the mountain environment they describe may be better appreciated. That is a characteristically modest statement, yet the reality is that his book breaks much completely new ground barely mentioned—if at all—in the District Guides. Examples are the major opening chapters on the Physical Description of the area (including present climate), the Origin of the Highlands (geology, past climate and geomorphology), on Colonization by Plant and Animal Life after the glaciers retreated, and on Man in the Highlands, which occupy almost half the main text of the book. Though dealing with technical subjects, these chapters are easy to read and are a special tribute to the author's abilities as a writer. The book would be well worth buying for them alone. The one on Origin is a very fine 20-page summary; no climber will look at the Scottish hills—or indeed hills anywhere—in the same way again after reading it. I spotted a few incorrect details in the chapter on plants and animals, but it would be unjustifiable to give prominence to them by mentioning them, when the chapter as a whole is so well done. Hilary and H. J. B. Birks contribute a special five pages on Scottish mountain plants, which is particularly good in not just giving the usual account of which species are there, but in explaining the much more interesting topic of why they come to be there.

The chapter on Man in the Highlands is especially welcome. Too often, we see books by climbers who use the Scottish hills for their recreation, but who are completely oblivious of the local people that live there and of the profound changes in social culture, language, population and land use which have contributed so much to producing the hill landscape that we see today. The author gives an excellent summary of the social history, starting with mesolithic man and finishing with the clearances and the crofters' revolt. He brings it right up to date by sympathetic accounts on emigration, the current social and economic problems of the Highlands, on hydro-electric power and minerals. Finally he discusses the future, emphasising the increasing conflicts between short-term, largely unplanned development on one hand, and the long-term conservation of the outstanding landscape and other natural resources of the Highlands on the other.

There follow five chapters on different regions: Southern, Central, West and Northern Highlands and the Cairngorms. Such short chapters on big areas, giving detail sufficient to be useful, could in other hands easily have become tedious pot-boiling summaries of the relevant District Guides. However, the author knows his Highlands well and is such a good writer that the chapters flow very well, even though packed with information. The best test is to read about the region one knows best, in my own case The Cairngorms; I found that chapter a pleasure to read.

One of the best chapters in this fine book is on the Development of Mountaineering, about 30 pages on the history of mountaineering in Scotland. Enthusiastic, analytical, and nowhere too parochial, it is unquestionably the best summary of the subject yet written. The only thing it lacks is a little on the human character behind the names of the various leading climbers, groups and clubs. A very good, though all too short, 4-page chapter follows on the Development of Scottish ski-ing.

There still remain over 60 pages packed with information. First, the author gives a very useful Bibliography, then a series of Appendices giving a list of all the Munros, the Mountain Code for Scotland, an account of the Mountaineering Council for Scotland and all its member clubs, the Outdoor Activities Centres, the names, addresses and functions of public and voluntary bodies concerned with the Highlands, a summary on mountain rescue, and a useful glossary of Gaelic and Norse words and place names. The last of the eight Appendices, on Access, exaggerates the damage done to grouse shooting and deer shooting by the passage of a walker. However, this in no way detracts from the author's recommendation that walkers should try to avoid unnecessary contact with deer shooting and grouse shooting, by asking for permission before they visit the hill during the shooting seasons.

To sum up, this book is a new and big event in the long history of fine publications by the S.M.C. It fully lives up to the importance of the event, and is undoubtedly a best buy.

ADAM WATSON.

Hamish's Mountain Walk.—(The first non-stop climb of all the Scottish Munros). By Hamish M. Brown. (1978; Gollancz. 353 pages. 51 photographs, 15 sketch maps. £7·50).

Sandy Cousins finishes his long happy days with a Drambuie and a cigar; Hamish Brown with a chapter of the Gospel.

And well he might. We all know of Hamish's pleasures, from cheery articles on ben and bothy in Scottish periodicals to jolly tales of chaps and gels in the Eagle Ski Club Journal. Here is his grossest hedonism yet.

In his vespers I hope he remembers old men who, passion spent for rubbing noses on rock and ice, restrained by Vichy's motto 'travail, famille,' still lust vicariously for such an excess of physical contact with the contours of *ciche* and *mhaighdean*. This book will sit easier on their fireside laps than *Hard Rock*—or *Playboy*. I was very pleased, then, when the Editor thrust it at me. 'This should interest *you*. Review it.' I have not yet come to terms with paying so much for such pleasures.

The great account flows well. There is no dwelling on the statistics of the march, no impression of dreary footslog. There is no moralising. Hamish chats as he moves along just as a new hill companion should. You learn of unknown corners and distant howffs. You pick up tips and hints. You hear jokes and snatches of gossip. You know what he likes to eat. You get to know him.

Plenty anecdote, history and legend, too, mix agreeably with the journal of day-to-day progress. We are given Munro and his pals, our own pals, the Clearances, the Lairds and the Forestry Commission, the Prince in the heather and the equally harassed Ripley brothers. You catch the great pleasures of our hills in Spring and early Summer—the birdsong, the deer, the fox, the exquisite solitary enjoyment of dawn and sunset. You share the anticipation and apprehension of the start in Mull, some of the middle anxiety about the feasibility of it all, the real, but brief, depression in Glen Dessary, the impatient excitement as he strides the last miles in Sutherland, the sadness, almost on Ben Hope. You read eagerly of hills known and hills desired. He invoked a special jealous interest as he approached my Aberdeenshire hills. All well done.

The photographs and sketch maps are good, the appendices, bibliography and list of addresses useful. The pronunciation and meaning of many Gaelic hill names are given en route (S.M.C. guidebooks please copy).

I squirmed only once or twice. I approve his regular personal hygiene. But washing *undies*? All this *and* knickers? Probably not. I found, too, that my prejudices made me skip doggy reminiscences and memories of Braehead loons.

But a delightful book. Happy, frank, unashamed, gloating. It ends with Hamish dashing off for a holiday in the Cuillin. There is no repentance.

M.T.

The Living Mountain.—By Nan Shepherd. (Aberdeen University Press. 95 pp. £2·50).

This modestly presented little book is subtitled 'A celebration of the Cairngorm Mountains of Scotland,' and rightly so. Any mountain lover will find pleasure and reward in reading it, especially if he knows the Cairngorms. Nan Shepherd is writing about perception—of water, air, rocks, light, plants and so on, and as such she tells us little that many of us do not already know or have experienced. However she writes so well, with such evocative sensitivity and vivid imagery, that one's own awareness of the mountain environment cannot avoid being enriched and reinforced. In a sense this book is a form of prose poetry and if you think poetry is not particularly to your taste, then try this. You may be pleasantly surprised.

W.D.B.

The Encyclopedia of Mountaineering.—By Walt Unsworth. (1977; Penguin. 397 pp, 1,000+ entries. £1·50).

To do full justice to a title like this is, of course, an ambitious if not an impossible task, even without the limitation of an inexpensive paperback format. Inevitably the author has had to be selective and understandably his selection is from the standpoint of an English climber. From a Scottish viewpoint there are gaps and inadequacies; we have references to Raeburn and Smith but not to Bell or Marshall, to the Etive Slabs but not Creag an Dubh Loch, to Arran but not Torridon. However, this is a useful book which represents a considerable amount of work. Especially practical are the guidebook and other references which accompany the entries on climbing areas. It abounds in interesting little snippets which jog the memory or arouse one's curiosity. Well worth the outlay, even if you only use it to accumulate the wherewithal to win pints in the pub.

W.D.B.

Walking and Climbing.—By Walt Unsworth. (1977; Routledge and Kegan Paul. 72 pp. £2·95).

Within the last two or three years several books about hill-walking and climbing in Britain specifically written for young people have been produced by such well-known authors as Walt Unsworth, Mike Banks and Tony Greenbank (to mention a few). Presumably the intention is to capitalise on the large number of youngsters being introduced to the hills in school parties and other organised groups. Thirty years ago the handbook for young climbers in Britain was John Barford's *Climbing in Britain*; Walt Unsworth's book is very different. It is clearly written for a much younger age group (early teens), and it seems designed to arouse the interest, curiosity and enthusiasm of aspiring young climbers without answering all the questions and explaining all the techniques in detail. The book does however, go to some lengths to warn of the hazards of the hills, and it is well illustrated. A good present if you have a young nephew or niece showing an interest in the hills.

D.J.B.

The Photoguide to Mountains.—By Douglas Milner. (1977; Focal Press. 184 pp. £2·25).

Thirty years ago Douglas Milner published his book *Mountain Photography*, and I dare say that for hundreds of climbers this book was the standard guide to black and white photography in the mountains. Since then colour photography has almost completely superseded black and white, and there has been a revolution, too, in the cameras we use. *The Photoguide to Mountains* aims to bring the earlier work up to date, and in particular it has new material on colour photography. In the chapters dealing with composition, lighting, choice of viewpoint and pictorial work many of the guiding principles enunciated in the earlier book remain unchanged, and many of the diagrams in the earlier book appear again. In one respect I feel that the present book suffers by comparison with its predecessor, the illustrations are neither so striking nor so numerous as in *Mountain Photography*, and I think that they are rather disappointing. Nevertheless, for anyone who wants to do more than just point his camera at the nearest bit of mountain scenery to catch his attention and press the shutter knob, this book is well worth studying.

D.J.B.

Mountaineering for Beginners.—By Mike Banks. (1977; Seeley, Service. 92 pp. £3·50).

This is a competent introduction to the sport and contains plenty of sensible advice. However, the book has nothing to make it stand out from the large and increasing number of books on the same subject. Although a hardback, this seems a lot to pay for 90 pages and is certainly poor value when compared with Blackshaw's classic which is much more comprehensive and also cheaper.

D.J.

Great Gable, Wasdale and Eskdale.—By P. L. Fearnehough. (1977; Fell and Rock Climbing Club). **Pillar Group.**—By A. G. Gram. (1977; Fell and Rock Climbing Club). **Gogarth.**—By Alec Sharp. (1977; Climbers' Club).

In both the Gable and the Pillar guides, revision has been undertaken by the author of the previous edition. Apart from the inclusion of new climbs, both books have been left largely unaltered except for necessary changes arising from regrading and the elimination of aid. For example, among the recommended routes in the 1968 edition of the Pillar guide, *Scylla* moves down to Very Severe while *The Appian Way* and *Eros* move up to Hard Severe and Extremely Severe respectively. There are some twenty-five new climbs in the Pillar guide, nine of which are on the Rock itself while most of the rest are located on the crags of Scoatfell. The first and longest of these climbs is *The Greater Traverse*, a combination of *The Eightfold Way*, *The Link* (the last new climb to appear in the 1968 edition) and *The Girdle Traverse*, giving 1,800 feet of climbing from Shamrock right round to South-West Climb and the top of High Man. In the Gable group perhaps the most impressive new climb is *The Viking* on the Tophet Wall section of the Napes. On the other side of the mountain there have been several new climbs on the remote Gable Crag, and some worthwhile contributions have also been made on the Boat Howe Crags of Kirkfell and on Heron Crag in Eskdale.

The new Gogarth guide contains an almost overwhelming wealth of hard climbs. The style, format, and grading policies in the book are much as in the author's guide to Clogwyn du'r Arddu, and accordingly there is a considerable amount of information about each climb. Furthermore, alongside the adjectival grades in the Extreme band, there is an experimental open-ended numerical E grading (at present running from E1 up to E5); no doubt time and usage will expose the relative merits of the two systems. Following the route descriptions there is a short but interesting section on the pleasures and pitfalls of sea level traversing, and the book finishes with Ken Wilson's excellent photodiagrams of the main climbing areas. Over seventy new routes have been discovered here since the publication of Crew's guide in 1969, and so the author ends the very comprehensive historical section with the view that '. . . . it would be unwise to dismiss Gogarth as having little left to climb.'

R.J.A.

Journals of Kindred Clubs

The following journals have been received: La Montagne, Rivista Mensile, Appalachia, Sierra Club Bulletin, Alpine J., Polar Record, Cairngorm Club J., Tararua, New Zealand Alpine J., Canadian Alpine J., J. South African Mountain Club, Wierchy (Polish).

Alpine Journal, 1977.—A good journal to dip into, with much of interest. This conservative reviewer liked Longlands Valedictory Address with its musing on current mountaineering values. Our own H. M. Brown pops up in the Julian Alps—he gets around! Scott gives a matter-of-fact account of his splendid new route done on Mount McKinley with Haston. The value of the somewhat fashionable 'space' blankets as a survival aid is well and truly scotched by the tests of P. Marcus. It seems that a poly bag is better. Recommended reading.

Cairngorm Club Journal, 1977.—I enjoyed this issue. There are two well-researched articles, one on the possibility of glaciers in the Cairngorms in the last three centuries (see also a bit less fancied than the article which appeared in our *Journal*), and the other on the part that fauna have played in the naming of our mountains, also some pleasant poetry and more.

C.S.

Grampian Club Bulletin.—Golden Jubilee Issue, 1977. This issue marks 50 years of the Grampian Club and as such has a reminiscent tone. The historical record is fulfilled by a series of reviews of Club activities over the years, studded with references to incidents involving ascents, accidents, benightments and one occasion when the Club bus was roped down an icy Glen Isla road. The picture emerges of a club which is salvationist in flavour rather than ultramontane but which has continued to maintain a vigorous identity over the years.

W.D.B.

Oxford Mountaineering, 1976/77.—Much better written than most university club journals this contains the usual descriptions of difficult climbing—much of it in racy but still literate style. Some of the contributions suffer from being all too brief, an exception being a first winter ascent of The Sassolungo which conveys its epic moments very convincingly.

W.D.B.

Appalachia, 1977.—A journal devoted almost exclusively to local interests and conservation matters. The only article of mountaineering content is a reprint from the *American Alpine Journal* of the account of the 1976 ascent of Nanda Devi. There is a frighteningly serious article titled 'Its time to license hikers.' The writer did not suggest any suitable penalties for non-payment of one's licence fee.

I.F.

REVIEWS   331

The Canadian Alpine Journal, 1977.—This is a big, glossy and superbly produced journal. It is also rather dull as most of the articles are uninspiring accounts of first ascents on remote mountains where geography and access are more significant than the actual climbing. On a more familiar scale, and rather out of place, is a description by Bugs (*sic*) McKeith of a new 150 ft. grade III ice climb, described in detail down to the last 15 ft. which can be avoided by climbing a large log leaning against the pitch. Many Scottish winter climbs would be enlivened by such pitches which would have the additional advantage of always being in good condition for front-pointing.

C. D. GRANT.

New Zealand Alpine Journal, 1977.—An interesting and thoroughly well produced journal. Articles range from home land first ascents to expeditions in Patagonia, Pence, Alaska and the Himalayas. The latter is a review of an eight-man expedition which attempted Everest by the South Col route without the assistance of Sherpas. That the expedition failed to reach the summit is not important. Their experience can be summarised in the words of their leader—'To me, an expedition to Everest should be first and foremost an adventure.' An informative article on the difficulties of management and planning of national parks carries a warning which could well apply to this country. The author states that certain interests 'are in danger of being neglected because they apparently do not satisfy either the conservation objectives of the National Parks Act or the economic objectives of the tourist industry.'

I.F.

The Journal of The Mountain Club of South Africa, 1976.—It is doubtful whether the M.C.S.A. would allow the gradual attrition taking place in many mountainous areas of Scotland, Glencoe being only one immediate example. This is an old Club—its Journal was first published in 1894, but its membership is large, growing, and very conscious of the delicate balance of the environment. One reads, in 'Viva Vandalism' by T. Johnson, of the 3,000+ sites exhibiting ancient rock paintings, and how they are attacked by vandals using candle smoke, paint, and in one case where a rare painting was protected by bars—foam from a well-shaken bottle of soft drink. At the same time there is a huge increase in the numbers going into the wilderness areas of South Africa, partly because the Government is providing and promoting, and parallelling this, increased public awareness of mountains and mountaineering. The M.C.S.A. therefore faces the old (to us) dilemma; more people means possible exploitation of the wilds, a negation of the very reasons most of them leave the cities for in the first place. We hope they find a benevolent means of control.

Disgracefully ignorant of the nicer things about South Africa, this reviewer managed to work out that a 'beacon' was synonymous with a cairn, a 'nek' was a bealach, and 'hakie-busch' was to be avoided. Remaining unclear are terms such as 'dassie traverses,' 'dongas,' and 'wormholes,' big enough to crawl through on routes. Most huts have snakebite kits, which must make a change from midges. We enjoyed Hoare's articles on the Hindu Kush and the Himalaya (this Club gets around), including a photograph of unclimbed (and unnamed) peaks which had us scrabbling for a travel agent. Not so well written was the only article of home interest, a very wet ascent of Raven's Gully. When one climbs in S.A. in searing temperatures of, sometimes, up to 40°, one probably dreams of climbing wet, cold Scottish gullies wearing welly boots filled to the brim with ice cubes and clutching a choc ice in each hand.

An appreciation of John Muir rounds off the strong conservation feeling prevalent in the Journal. Well illustrated with 38 photographs, 4 in colour including two very good prints of the superb Snowflower, *Protea cryophila*, this is a respectably solid Journal.

K.V.C.

OFFICE BEARERS, 1977-78

Honorary President: ALEXANDER HARRISON, C.B.E.

President: JAMES C. DONALDSON, M.B.E.

Vice-Presidents: N. W. QUINN and C. C. GORRIE.

Hon. Secretary: D. J. BENNET, 4 Morven Road, Bearsden, Glasgow.
Hon. Treasurer: W. WALLACE, 22 Bonaly Terrace, Edinburgh. Hon.
Editor: W. D. BROOKER, 35 Oakhill Road, Aberdeen. Convener of
Publications Sub-Committee: G. J. TISO, 13 Wellington Place, Leith,
Edinburgh. Editor of District Guidebooks: A. C. D. SMALL, 13 Hollybush
Road, Crieff, Perthshire. Editor of Rock-Climbing Guidebooks: A. H.
HENDRY, 15 Lauderdale Street, Edinburgh. Hon. Librarian: A. C. STEAD,
544 Shields Road, Glasgow. Hon. Custodian of Slides: P. HODGKISS,
495 Clarkston Road, Glasgow. Hon. Meets Secretary: G. S. ROGER, Glen-
ranald, 1 Pendreich Road, Bridge of Allan, Perthshire. Convener of Huts
Sub-Committee: R. T. RICHARDSON, 2 Inchlonaig Drive, Balloch,
Dunbartonshire. Custodian of C.I.C. Hut: G. S. PEET, 6 Roman Way,
Dunblane, Perthshire. (Tel. 078 682 3954). Custodian of Lagangarbh:
J. CRAWFORD, 14 Rannoch Road, Wemyss Bay, Renfrewshire. Custodian of
Ling Hut: J. F. ANTON, Sandpipers, 1 Craigdarroch Drive, Contin, by
Strathpeffer, Ross-shire. Committee: The President, Vice-Presidents,
Hon. Secretary, Hon. Treasurer, Hon. Editor, Conveners of Publications and
Huts Sub-Committees (all as above) and H. M. BROWN, J. CRAWFORD,
K. V. CROCKET, B. FRASER, I. FULTON, C. D. GRANT, D. JENKINS,
W. H. JONES and K. MACRAE.

Journal Information

Distribution: D. F. LANG, 580 Perth Road, Dundee.
Advertisements: W. H. JONES, 88 Albany Road, Broughty Ferry.
New Routes Editor: K. V. CROCKET, Department of Zoology, University
                        of Glasgow.
Assistant Editor: I. H. M. SMART.
Editor: W. D. BROOKER, 35 Oakhill Road, Aberdeen.

All MSS should be submitted as soon as possible and at any rate before
the end of February. Articles and other lengthy contributions preferably typed
on one side of paper, DOUBLE-SPACED with inch margins. The editor
welcomes contributions from members, other Scottish mountaineers and from
foreign visitors (provided these last deal with some aspect of Scottish
mountains or mountaineering). Photographs are also welcome and should
be black and white unglazed glossy prints 6" by 8" or larger. All material
should be sent to the Editor, address as above.

ii.

all at sea
mountaineering?

Ever thought of using a very comfortable motor yacht as your base camp? Coming back after a good days climb to a hot shower, central heating, good food—then off to the next climb?

Such as Rhum; the peaks round Lochs Hourn, Nevis and Duich; the Cuillins from Loch Harport; the innumerable sea stacks and cliffs; or anywhere you want.

PENTLAND WAVE is a 70 ton converted MFV, fully equipped for comfort and safety. She sleeps 12 in two berth and single cabins, and operates all year round. Cost is from £80 per berth per week all in.

Details from:
TONY DALTON (SMJ), LOCHAVICH, TAYNUILT, ARGYLL

v.

SCOTTISH MOUNTAINEERING TRUST

DISTRICT
GUIDE
BOOKS

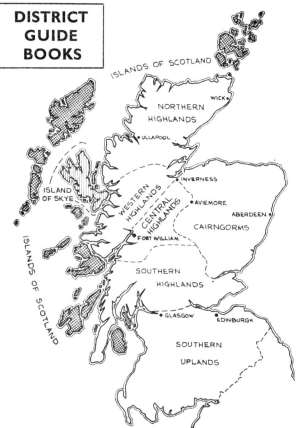

ISLANDS OF SCOTLAND

NORTHERN
HIGHLANDS

WICK

ULLAPOOL

ISLAND
OF SKYE

INVERNESS

WESTERN
HIGHLANDS

AVIEMORE

CENTRAL
HIGHLANDS

ABERDEEN

CAIRNGORMS

FORT WILLIAM

ISLANDS OF SCOTLAND

SOUTHERN
HIGHLANDS

GLASGOW

EDINBURGH

SOUTHERN

UPLANDS

AND AN ESSENTIAL ADDITION TO EVERY MOUNTAINEERS LIBRARY
THE SCOTTISH HIGHLANDS — W. H. MURRAY

CLIMBERS GUIDE BOOKS		
CUILLIN OF SKYE	2 vols.
GLENCOE and ARDGOUR	2 vols.
CAIRNGORMS AREA	3 vols.
NORTHERN HIGHLANDS	2 vols.
ARRAN	1 vol.
ARROCHAR	1 vol.
BEN NEVIS	1 vol.

NEW 4 COLOUR MAP OF THE BLACK CUILLIN

Published by the Scottish Mountaineering Club
Copyright © 1977 Scottish Mountaineering Club, Edinburgh
SBN 901516 84 8

**Distributed by West Col, Goring, Reading, Berks. RG8 0AP
also available from Mountaineering Book Sellers**

ix.

ON TOP OF THE WORLD
WITH NORTHCAPE

The British team selected North Cape Polar Wear for the first
British ascent of the Ogre. North Cape is the only 100%
Dacron Polar Wear—the experts' choice.

North Cape Textiles Limited, Berryden Mills,
6 Berryden Road, Aberdeen AB9 2WB
Telephone: (0224) 630357

·for the big outdoors·

xv.